Archetypal Process

Archetypal Process

Self and Divine in Whitehead,
Jung, and Hillman

EDITED BY DAVID RAY GRIFFIN

Northwestern University Press
Evanston, Illinois

Northwestern University Press
Evanston, Illinois 60201

Printed in the United States of America

Library of Congress Cataloging-in-Publication Data

Archetypal process : self and divine in Whitehead, Jung, and Hillman /
    edited by David Ray Griffin.
        p.   cm.
    Includes bibliographical references.
    ISBN 0-8101-0815-1.—ISBN 0-8101-0816-X (pbk.)
    1. Process philosophy. 2. Process theology. 3. Archetype
(Psychology) 4. Whitehead, Alfred North, 1861-1947. 5. Jung, C. G.
(Carl Gustav), 1875-1961. 6. Hillman, James. I. Griffin, David
Ray, 1939-   .
BD372.A73   1989
146'.7—dc20
                                                    89-12827
                                                        CIP

CONTENTS

PREFACE   vii

ABBREVIATIONS   ix

1. *Introduction* Archetypal Psychology and
Process Philosophy: Complementary
Postmodern Movements   DAVID RAY GRIFFIN   1

2. Jung and Whitehead on Self and Divine:
The Necessity for Symbol and Myth   GERALD H. SLUSSER   77

3. The Necessity for Symbol and Myth:
A Literary Amplification   J'NAN MORSE SELLERY   93

4. Inspiration and Creativity:
An Extension   GERALD H. SLUSSER   105

5. Once More:
The Cavern beneath the Cave   STANLEY R. HOPPER   107

6. Eternal Objects and Archetypes,
Past and Depth:
A Response to Stanley Hopper   JOHN B. COBB, JR.   125

7. Language as Metaphorical:
A Reply to John Cobb   STANLEY R. HOPPER   129

8. Psychocosmetics and the
Underworld Connection   CATHERINE KELLER   133

9. Psychocosmetics:
A Jungian Response   ROBERT L. MOORE   157

10. Reconnecting:
A Reply to Robert Moore   CATHERINE KELLER   163

11. The Mystique of the Nonrational
and a New Spirituality   JAMES W. HEISIG   167

12. Imaginal Soul and Ideational Spirit:
A Response to James Heisig   CHARLES E. WINQUIST   203

13. A Riposte   JAMES W. HEISIG   209

14. Back to Beyond: On Cosmology   JAMES HILLMAN   213

15. Back of "Back to Beyond"
and Creeping Dichotomism   EDWARD S. CASEY   233

16. A Metaphysical Psychology to
Un-Locke Our Ailing World   DAVID RAY GRIFFIN   239

17. Responses   JAMES HILLMAN   251

NOTES ON CONTRIBUTORS   267

NOTES   269

INDEX   285

PREFACE

The terms "process" and "archetypal" in the title refer to two movements: the process theology derived primarily from Alfred North Whitehead, and the archetypal psychology derived primarily from Carl Gustav Jung but so named by James Hillman, who has also introduced some modifications—some would say heresies—into the movement.

These two movements share many ideas and fundamental aims. In particular, they both want to return soul and divinity to the world (hence the subtitle of this book). Is it possible for them to join forces against the soul-denying and divinity-excluding materialisms and positivisms that they both oppose? Can archetypalists derive cosmological depth, breadth, and support from process theology? Can process theologians acquire a developed, empirically based psychology and a richer, more evocative rhetoric of soul and divinity from archetypalists? More modestly: can people rooted in one of these two movements genuinely converse with those from the other? Or are the differences in fundamental intention and approach between the *philosophical* and *psychologizing* modes of thought so profound as to make genuine dialogue, let alone conspiracy, impossible?

These were the questions underlying, and providing both the excitement for and apprehension about, a conference organized by the Center for Process Studies, and held at Claremont University Center and Graduate School in March of 1983. Although James Hillman was the figure around whom the conference was organized, it was decided to bring process theology into dialogue equally with the thought of both Jung and Hillman. The present book arises out of that conference, although many of the contributions, including the introduction and Hillman's concluding response, have been written since the conference, specifically for this book. The question that lay behind the conference—whether these two traditions can be married, or even engaged—which is developed in the introduction, can also be traced through many of the essays.

I have many thanks to give: to Claremont University Center and Graduate School, and the School of Theology at Claremont, whose support for the Center for Process Studies made both the conference and this book possible; to Catherine Keller, who at the time of the conference was a Ph.D. student in Claremont, and who not only did much of the drudge work, with which graduate students usually get stuck, but also suggested the idea for the conference and did much of the planning for it; to the Jung Club of Claremont for their help with the conference; to John Cobb and Nancy Howell for taking over most of my duties at the Center to allow me time to complete this book; to all the contributors, especially James Hillman, whose generous, undogmatic, and witty spirit (perhaps I should say soul) set the tone for a conference in which genuine conversation, the growth of mutual understanding and appreciation, and even movement of thought, occurred; to Marcia Doss and the secretaries at the School of Theology, especially Stephanie Graham, for helping me almost meet deadlines; to my wife for divine patience and soulful support; to Jonathan Brent and Susan Harris of Northwestern University Press for their enthusiastic support of this book; and to their excellent copy editor, Sally Serafim. With regard to the introductory essay, I am indebted for good advice to many people, especially Charles Asher, John Cobb, James Hillman, Ann Jaqua, Catherine Keller, and Stanley Hopper. Although some of them replied affirmatively to my query as to whether it should be greatly abbreviated, others said no. The decision to accept the latter counsel is, of course, one for which I alone am finally responsible—regardless of how much it may have been influenced by some deep archetype.

ABBREVIATIONS FOR WRITINGS OF WHITEHEAD, JUNG, AND HILLMAN

Page references to the writings of Alfred North Whitehead, Carl Jung, and James Hillman are included parenthetically in the text. Below is a list of the abbreviations of those of their works that are cited and the editions of the writings to which they refer.

Works Cited by Alfred North Whitehead

AI   *Adventures of Ideas* (New York: Free Press, 1967).

D   *Dialogues of Alfred North Whitehead*, recorded by Lucien Price (New York: Mentor, 1964).

ESP   *Essays in Science and Philosophy* (New York: Philosophical Library, 1947).

FR   *The Function of Reason* (Boston: Beacon Press, 1967).

MT   *Modes of Thought* (New York: Free Press, 1968).

PR   *Process and Reality: An Essay in Cosmology,* corrected edition, ed. David Ray Griffin and Donald W. Sherburne (New York: Free Press, 1978).

RM   *Religion in the Making* (Cleveland and New York: World Publishing Co., Meridian Books, 1960).

S   *Symbolism: Its Meaning and Effect* (New York: G. P. Putnam's Sons, Capricorn Books, 1959).

SMW   *Science and the Modern World* (New York: Free Press, 1967).

Works Cited by Carl Jung

CW   *Collected Works,* in twenty volumes, ed. Herbert Read, Michael Fordham, and Gerhard Adler (London: Routledge & Kegan Paul, 1953–78). References cite volume and paragraph, not page, unless otherwise indicated.

L   *Letters,* ed. Gerhard Adler and Aniela Jaffe (Princeton: Princeton University Press, 1973).

MDR   *Memories, Dreams, Reflections,* ed. Aniela Jaffe, trans. Richard and Clara Winston (New York: Random House, 1963).

MMSS   *Modern Man in Search of a Soul* (New York: Harcourt Brace Jovanovich, 1966).

Works Cited by James Hillman

AP   *Archetypal Psychology: A Brief Account* (Dallas: Spring Publications, 1983).

DU   *The Dream and the Underworld* (New York: Harper & Row, 1979).

FG   *Facing the Gods* (ed.) (Dallas: Spring Publications, 1980).

HF   *Healing Fiction* (Barrytown, N.Y.: Station Hill Press, 1983).

I   *Insearch: Psychology and Religion* (New York: Charles Scribner's Sons, 1967; Dallas: Spring Publications, 1979).

JT   *Lectures on Jung's Typology* (with M.-L. von Franz) (New York and Zurich: Spring Publications, 1971).

LE   *Loose Ends: Primary Papers in Archetypal Psychology* (Dallas: Spring Publications, 1975).

MA   *The Myth of Analysis: Three Essays in Archetypal Psychology* (New York: Harper & Row, 1978).

PP   *Puer Papers* (Dallas: Spring Publications, 1979).

RVP   *Re-Visioning Psychology* (New York: Harper & Row, 1975).

S 19—   *Spring: An Annual of Archetypal Psychology and Jungian Thought* (issues are cited by year, e.g., *S 1980*).

SS   *Suicide and the Soul* (New York: Harper & Row, 1974; Dallas: Spring Publications, 1976).

TH   *The Thought of the Heart* (Dallas: Spring Publications, 1981).

1

INTRODUCTION

Archetypal Psychology and Process Theology

Complementary Postmodern Movements

DAVID RAY GRIFFIN

The thesis of this introduction is that *archetypal psychology*, meaning that movement originating with Carl Jung (1875–1961) and so named by James Hillman, and *process theology*, meaning that movement originating with Alfred North Whitehead (1861–1947), are both postmodern movements, and that they are complementary, with each providing things the other needs. The possibility behind this book as a whole, implicit in its title, *Archetypal Process*, is that these two postmodern movements might in a sense join forces, thereby strengthening each other and providing a common front against the deadening trajectory of late modernity, which threatens the life of the individual with meaninglessness and the life of the planet with destruction.

I develop this thesis in the following order. In the first section, I discuss the key terms: *archetypal psychology, process theology, complementarity, modern,* and *postmodern.* The second section summarizes a number of postmodern points shared by Whitehead and Jung; the third discusses some of their major differences and the question of whether these differences prevent a collaboration. In the fourth section, I suggest some of the things that process theologians can acquire from archetypal psychology. In the fifth through ninth sections, I deal with the difficult question of whether Whiteheadian process theology could provide a framework, more adequate than that provided by Jung himself, for the central insights and concerns of archetypal psychology. The topics of these sections are nonsensory perception and the mind-body problem, parapsychology and life after death, the origin of archetypes, the divine reality, and method in science and philosophy. In the tenth section, I point to questions that arise in relation to James Hillman's distinctive form of archetypal psychology. In the final section, I provide a preview of some of the issues discussed in the essays herein.

I should say at the outset that this introduction does not pretend to be written from a neutral or transcendent perspective. Although I have been greatly informed and enlarged by my encounter with archetypal psychology, I approach the question of the relation between the two movements with the sensibilities, interests, and biases of an advocate of process theology. With regard to the issues on which the two movements have differed thus far, therefore, I generally see greater wisdom in the process position, and give arguments in its support. My perspective even has determined the topics chosen for discussion and the style in which they are discussed. An introduction to the essays in this volume written by a participant in the archetypal tradition would be much different in form, style, and content.

I. Discussion of Key Terms

The choice of the term "archetypal psychology" requires comment. The accepted term for the Jungian movement has long been "analytical psychology." To use "archetypal" instead is to accept James Hillman's judgment that this term better suggests the central and distinctive emphasis of this movement (LE 142). Use of this term does introduce a note of ambiguity, to be sure, because "archetypal psychology" is also the term for that somewhat post-Jungian movement led by Hillman himself which diverges from Jung's ideas on some important issues. Because this book is about both Jungian psychology in general and also Hillman's distinctive version of it, the term "archetypal psychology" in this introduction has two meanings: a generic meaning, referring to Jungian thought in general, especially Jung's own thought, and a more specific meaning, referring to Hillman's thought with its distinctive emphases. The generic meaning is used until section X.

The choice of the term "process theology" for the movement arising from the inspiration of Alfred North Whitehead also requires comment. Whitehead developed his position while teaching in the philosophy department at Harvard University, and he referred to his own thought as philosophy. He generally called it the "philosophy of organism" but, partly because his major work was entitled *Process and Reality,* the term that caught on was "process philosophy." However, a doctrine of God is central to this philosophy; *Process and Reality,* in fact, grew out of Whitehead's Gifford Lectures, the assigned topic for which is "natural theology," which means a philosophical theology—a theology derived from reflection on experiences generally available to human beings. The term "process theology" has, accordingly, become widely used for this philosophy, especially when the chief focus is on God and other questions of "ultimate concern" (Paul Tillich), such as ultimate origin, order, value, and meaning. Sometimes, to be sure, the term "process theology" refers to the use of this philosophical theology to understand ideas unique to a particular tradition, such as Torah in Judaism, christology in Christianity, or nirvana in Buddhism. But here the term refers to the more generic features of process thought, especially that of Whitehead himself. In any case, the term "theology" does not indicate that "faith" in some "special revelation" is presupposed. The criteria appealed to are the normal criteria of philosophical acceptability: self-consistency, adequacy to experienced facts, and illuminating power.

Just as it is natural to make the question of the divine central to a discussion of process philosophy, the same is true of archetypal psychology. As James Heisig says in *Imago Dei,* which is subtitled *A Study of C. G. Jung's Psychology of Religion,* the religious aspect of Jung's thought is so central "that it has become the typical turning point for sympathy or alienation from Jung's life and work."[1] Jung himself said: "The decisive question for man is: Is he related to something infinite or not?" (*MDR* 325). And one of Jung's most quoted statements is: "Among all my patients in the second half of life . . . there has not been one whose problem in the last resort was not that of finding a religious outlook on life" (*CW* 11:509).

One might well wonder if the present approach promises anything new. The literature discussing Jung's thought theologically is already considerable. And, at the close of a thorough bibliographical essay on this literature in 1973, Heisig said: "scholarship on the borderlands between theology and archetypal psychology has grown tired."[2] This was not, however, a plea to end the discussion. Instead, Heisig said: "What it needs . . . is . . . the painstaking re-examination of fundamental assumptions." Heisig himself contributed to this reexamination in the aforementioned *Imago Dei,* which appeared in 1979 and is still the most comprehensive and intelligent study of the subject. Based on a familiarity with the entire range of the Jungian corpus, including unpublished lectures as well as the secondary literature, this book should be presupposed by any study that hopes to make an advance.

My approach is to suggest that the two movements, process theology and archetypal psychology, are *complementary*. On the one hand, they have much in common, so that a dialogue between them can begin with many shared convictions. On the other hand, they focus on different issues, come at them from quite different perspectives, and accordingly have different strengths, with each supplying things the other lacks. A mutual appropriation of elements from the other could therefore be mutually beneficial. The resulting position could be far stronger than either movement by itself as hitherto developed.

There is nothing new, to be sure, about suggesting a complementarity between theology and Jungian psychology: this suggestion has been made countless times. Any novelty, and therefore promise for advance, lies in the particular theology in question, namely process theology. Most of the previous theological treatments of Jung's thought have been carried out either from the perspective of a nonphilosophical theology, based on an appeal to special revelation, or else from the perspective of a more traditional philosophical theology, especially Thomism. Process theology, by contrast, is a philosophical theology, one that was developed at the same time as Jung's own thought, and one that is, like it, evolutionary through and through. Thus far very little work has been done in relating the two—the most thorough study to date (to my knowledge) being a preliminary paper, "Whitehead and the Jungian Archetypes," written by Heisig in 1978 but never published.[3] An exploration between archetypal psychologists and process theologians may therefore open up some unplowed ground, and some of it may prove to be fertile.

By referring to both movements as *postmodern* I indicate that they reject many of the central tenets of the modern worldview, which began coming to dominance in the seventeenth and eighteenth centuries through the influence of Galileo, Mersenne, Descartes, Boyle, Hobbes, Newton, Locke, Hume, and related thinkers. Characteristic of this modern outlook were these three doctrines: (1) a *mechanistic doctrine of nature*, according to which natural things are wholly devoid of sentience, experience, or interiority, of any power of self-determination or "final causation," and of any power to act or be affected at a distance: all causation is efficient causation, and there is no action at a distance—all efficient causation is by contact and therefore between contiguous (touching) events (Newton's "gravitation" seemed to be an exception, which is precisely why it was so controversial and why Newton went positivistic on this point, saying that he made no causal hypotheses but provided only a descriptive mathematical formula); (2) *sensate empiricism*, according to which all knowledge originates in sensory perception, so that all extrasensory or nonsensory perception is denied (which follows from the assertion that all causal influence occurs between contiguous events); and (3) *a denial of any divine presence*, especially any *present divine influence*, in the world.

In its first exponents, with the exception of Hobbes, the modern worldview was *dualistic*, distinguishing the human soul radically from "nature," and *supernaturalistic*, thinking of nature and human souls as having been created *ex nihilo* by an omnipotent deity, who imposed motion and order on nature and implanted moral, religious, and aesthetic values in the human soul. Although Newton believed that God, besides acting thus at the beginning, also intervened in the world from time to time, the first version of modern thought quickly became deistic, saying that God exerted no further influence in the world after the initial act of creating it. In the latter half of the eighteenth century, God and the soul began disappearing, leaving *atheistic materialism* as the dominant outlook of the scientific community and eventually of the majority of the cultural elite. The loss of God and the soul meant that the mechanistic view, which was previously restricted to the nonhuman creation, now applied to the universe as a whole (which could no longer be thought of as "creation"). With this development, not only was nature disenchanted—stripped of all purpose, interiority, enjoyment, and "magic" (events involving action at a distance), but also the world as a whole was disenchanted—stripped of all purpose, meaning, and objective values.

By the beginning of the twentieth century, this "scientific materialism" was the reigning orthodoxy. This worldview had devastating implications for psychology, for parapsychology (which, as discussed below, is of great significance to archetypal psychology), and for theology. The implication for *psychology* was that it, like every other discipline, had to rest on a materialistic basis to be respectable. The implication for *parapsychology* (which was then called "psychical research") was that it could not possibly be a respectable enterprise, because the types of events it seeks to study could not possibly occur: extrasensory perception was excluded by the sensationist doctrine of perception; psychokinesis was excluded by the rejection of the soul as something distinct from the brain with causal power of its own; and both were excluded by the denial of any causal influence at a distance. The third main area of parapsychology, evidence for human survival of bodily death, was excluded by the materialistic denial of anything about the human being that could possibly survive this event. Scientific materialism also implied that *theology* could not be a respectable discipline: religious belief (in God, in objective values, in immortality, even in freedom) could not possibly correspond to anything real, but had to be explained as an illusion or pathology, or at best in purely functional terms.

"Individualism" is perhaps the word most often used to sum up modernity, and we can see its aptness from the foregoing account. The "elementary particles" of nature were said to be self-enclosed atoms, having only external relations with their environment—no internal relations in which the environment would be partially constitutive of them. And about the same was said of the human being. The sensationist doctrine of perception said that nothing could enter the human mind except through the individual's bodily senses, and then "sensation" was so defined that nothing of the external world actually entered the mind to become constitutive of it: the mind simply had "sense-data," which in some mysterious way "represented" the outer things. And the closedness of the world to divine influence completed this insistence on autonomy understood as the absence of internal relatedness.

Whitehead and Jung are postmodern in that they both, albeit with different emphases, reject these tenets of the modern worldview, yet without returning to a premodern approach. They retain the formal commitment of modernity to rational empiricism, but they reject some of the substantive presuppositions of modernity.

I should perhaps point out that my use of "postmodern" is quite different from its dominant use in artistic, literary, and deconstructive philosophical circles. That type of postmodernism should really be called *ultra*modernism, or *most*modernism, because it results from taking some of the presuppositions of modernity to their logical conclusions. In contrast with this relativistic, nihilistic, deconstructive postmodernism, I speak of a constructive, reconstructive, or revisionary postmodernism, in which many of the presuppositions of modernity are challenged and revised. I have developed these ideas elsewhere.[4]

I now turn to the point that Whitehead and Jung are both postmodern thinkers and share many postmodern convictions. It is noteworthy that both wrote books with "modern" in the title: Whitehead's *Science and the Modern World* was matched by Jung's *Modern Man in Search of a Soul*. Neither one used the *term* "postmodern," but the *idea* of going beyond the modern is central to each of them. The notion that Jung is a postmodern psychologist, incidentally, has been suggested by Peter Homans, who speaks of "the modern and post-modern facet of Jung's thought."[5] Although Jung exemplifies all three of Peter Berger's categories of modernization, counter-modernization and demodernization, Homans says, he mainly embodies the third.

> He did indeed counsel a return to the past, but only in order that the past might be surpassed. . . . [T]he emergence of the self, the final state of the individuation process, while it is built in part upon modernizing and counter-modernizing processes, also attempts to go beyond these in the direction of demodernization, a view of the person which is entirely new, being neither simply modern nor simply traditional.[6]

The idea that Whitehead is a postmodern thinker is one that I develop at length elsewhere.[7]

II. Postmodern Ideas
Shared by Whitehead and Jung

Jung and Whitehead share many postmodern beliefs. I will briefly point to some of the most important ones.

Both thinkers make the psyche or soul central. Both treat it as real—in fact as that thing or process of whose reality we are most certain. Jung says, in a statement Whitehead would endorse: "It is indeed paradoxical that . . . the psyche should be treated as if it were only semi-existent. Psychic existence is the only category of existence of which we have *immediate* knowledge" (*CW* 11:769). Whitehead says that "the percipient occasion is its own standard of actuality" (*PR* 145). Both men regard the psyche as distinct from the brain, and as having power of its own. They both, in fact, regard the human soul as the most powerful of all earthly creatures.

This rejection of the reductionistic materialism of later modernity is not accomplished, however, by a return to the dualism of early modernity. Both men—although Whitehead is much more clear and consistent on this point—suggest that the ultimate stuff of the world, called "energy" by Jung and "creativity" by Whitehead, is the source equally of what we ordinarily call the "physical" and the "mental." Everything, from electrons to the human psyche, embodies this creative energy. Something analogous to human experience must be present, then, in the entities studied by physics: modernity's mechanistic, anti-animistic doctrine of nature is rejected.

The sensate empiricism of modernity is likewise rejected, and on this point Jung and Whitehead are equally adamant. Empiricism is still embraced, but the equation of perception with *sensory* perception is rejected. The entire system of each thinker is based on the reality, in fact the primacy, of nonsensory perception.

Whereas sensory perception is based on data transmitted through a chain of contiguous events, nonsensory perception allows for the possibility of receiving influences from a distance. The "distance" in question can be either spatial distance, which the phrase "action at a distance" usually suggests, or temporal distance: the unmediated reception of influence from events in the more or less remote past. Both men affirm the reality of occurrences that lie open to such an interpretation—and here it is Jung who is the most explicit: his theories of "synchronicity" and "archetypes" are both based on such occurrences. The question of whether such events are indeed to be interpreted as instances of causal influence at a distance, however, is complex and will be explored later.

The possibility of action at a distance, combined with the earlier point about the power of the human soul, provides a basis for accepting psychokinesis, the psyche's direct influence on physical objects beyond one's own body. Such events were pivotal in Jung's own life and were mentioned often in his writings. Whitehead did not mention psychokinesis (at least in his published writings), but he does explicitly allow for extrasensory perception, and in his position perception and causal influence are simply the reverse sides of the same thing. To allow for perception at a distance is thereby to allow for efficient causation at a distance.

Their affirmations of the distinct reality and power of the human soul, and its capacity to perceive and act in extrabodily ways, also led both thinkers to affirm the theoretical possibility of life after death. Although it seems that only Jung actually believed in its reality, the most important point is that both positions provide a basis for looking seriously at the empirical evidence.

Their affirmation of nonsensory perception led them to reject the individualism of modernity. Far from being a self-enclosed monad, the human psyche is largely constituted by its reception of influences from the past world. This is Jung's "collective unconscious," of course, but Whitehead is no less emphatic on the point: far from, like one of Descartes's substances, requiring nothing but itself to be what it is, each soul requires its whole past world to be what it is. In some way or another, it incorporates that past within itself. And this past is present, both men agree, in an active, living way.

The affirmation of nonsensory perception leads to yet another important similarity between Jung and Whitehead: the rejection of an antithesis between ideas and feelings. "In the place of the Hegelian hierarchy of categories of thought" Whitehead puts "a hierarchy of categories of feeling" (*PR* 166). Accordingly, besides bodily and other low-grade feelings, there are propositional feelings and various types of intellectual feelings: "Understanding is a special form of feeling" (*PR* 143). The notion of "pure thought" is therefore "a figment of the learned world. A thought is a tremendous mode of excitement" (*MT* 36). Some ideas, of course, evoke more excitement than others, and one of the remarkable features of life—remarkable at least given modernity's materialism and sensationism—is that some ideas are seen as having great "importance" (*MT* 11–12). One form of importance is the sense of holiness (*MT* 120). Whitehead's discussion here is parallel to Jung's focus on "numinous" ideas.

Jung's whole psychology, in fact, developed from the notion of "complexes" in which ideas, images, and emotions were inextricably intertwined. The reason that the rejection of sensationism is important for recognizing this point is that in conscious sensory perception the emotional nature of the datum is largely lost. In seeing the tree before me, for example, I have a clear visual idea or image of the tree but no feeling of any feelings enjoyed by the tree itself. This leads me to, in Martin Buber's terms, a purely I-It relation to the tree. The same is true of my sensory perception of another person; this can at most lead to an imaginative identification with her or his feelings. But in nonsensory perception, which Whitehead called "perception in the mode of causal efficacy," or simply "prehension," I directly receive the emotional feelings that had been experienced by the datum. For example, in feeling an injured part of my body, I feel it by sharing *its* pain. Whitehead in fact called this kind of perception or feeling a "conformal" feeling, because the subject's feelings are conformed to the feelings transmitted by the objects felt. This notion will be presupposed in the later discussion of how to explain the power of archetypes.

The rejection of individualism and the affirmation of the massive influence of the past did not lead either thinker, however, to reject the importance of freedom and individuality. Each man thought of the soul as dipolar: besides the pole labeled "collective" (Jung) or "physical" (Whitehead), there is also the "personal" or "mental" pole, in which the person's freedom and therefore individuality can be expressed. This is all-important: intrinsic value resides only in individuals, not in collectives. And the potential intrinsic values of the individual can be realized only by transcending the collective attitudes and responses and by developing one's unique capacities—by "individuating," to use Jung's term. Whitehead says that social orders should be evaluated "according to their success in magnifying the individual actualities, that is to say, in promoting strength of experience" (*AI* 376).

While this distinction between the impersonal and personal poles of the soul is not quite identical with the relation between the unconscious and conscious portions, it is closely related. For both men the nonsensory reception of influence is primarily unconscious, while freedom or self-determination is primarily correlated with consciousness. And, although each thinker is sobering about the degree to which all thought and even perception are conditioned by unconscious processes, neither accepts the complete determination of conscious by unconscious processes. Even if Jung sometimes seems to say otherwise, he, like Whitehead, denies that consciousness is merely epiphenomenal, regarding it instead as finally decisive (*MDR* 187).

Implicit in this discussion has been the rejection of further aspects of the modern view of causation. Of the Aristotelian four causes, I have already mentioned both men's rejection of modernity's limitation of efficient causation to contiguous events, and its limitation of material causation to the energy embodied in the entities studied by physics (as each affirms a greatly expanded notion of energy or "creativity"). But modernity also had a very limited notion of formal causation: the forms embodied in things were limited to mathematical forms. And final causation, or teleology, was eliminated altogether.

Jung and Whitehead both reassert something like the Platonic view of the importance of formal causes in the nature of things. Jung does this, of course, by making archetypes central. The technical term for formal causes in Whitehead's thought is "eternal objects," and he explicitly affirms that, besides eternal objects of the objective species (the mathematical Platonic forms), there are also eternal objects of the subjective species (*PR* 291), which include anything that can qualify the subjective form of a feeling, such as emotions. But also the whole panoply of metaphysical principles, which Whitehead calls the "categoreal scheme" (*PR* 18–29), must be regarded as eternal formal causes of everything that occurs. Whitehead refused John Dewey's demand that he choose between a "genetic-functional" and a "mathematical-formal" account of the world, saying that the task was to fuse the two (*ESP* 123).

Finalism or teleology is equally affirmed by both. One of Jung's major divergences from Freud was due to the latter's attempt to explain all human experience in terms of efficient causes, whereas Jung became convinced that our aim toward the future—our aim to individuate, or realize our Self—was equally important. Whitehead equates "mentality" with final causation, meaning self-determination in terms of a momentary goal, so his ascription of a "mental pole" to each actual entity is an ascription of final causation to all actualities. He in fact says that each actual entity embodies a "subjective aim." These aims can be of greatly varying degrees. In low-grade entities, such as electrons and atoms, they would be mere "physical purposes," blind urges to realize some simple form of value in the present and immediate future. In human experience, one's aim, while rooted in blind urges received from the body and the past, can become enlightened by consciousness, and can be concerned about values in the remote future and for the world as a whole.

This discussion of the self and its purposes brings us to the question of God. Both Jung and Whitehead, who received their university education in the latter half of the nineteenth century, became radically agnostic about God if not atheistic, and both remained highly critical of the traditional doctrine of God to the end, believing it both false and harmful. But both, as they thought through the implications of their postmodern positions and the persistent facts of human experience, came to speak positively of God—albeit a God very different from that of traditional theism. And, although Jung's and Whitehead's discussions of God diverged radically (I will explore this issue later), both of them connected God to the teleology inherent in experience. For Whitehead, God is the source of the initial phase of the subjective aim. For Jung, the *imago dei* was equated, at least at times, with the individuated Self toward which the psyche is aiming. Talk of God was, therefore, for each man associated with the formal cause that is the individual's ideal final cause.

This final cause of the person was also understood in a similar way by Jung and Whitehead. The aim of life is to achieve depth and intensity of experience (while also maintaining a tolerable harmony). Jung first opposed religion because of its close connection, in his mind, with a moralism that prevented the achievement of depth; and as he became more positive toward religion he still opposed "faith" for this reason (*MDR* 94).[8] Whitehead said that the "ultimate creative purpose" is that each experience shall achieve "some maximum depth of intensity of feeling" (*PR* 249). "The primordial appetitions which jointly constitute God's purpose are seeking intensity"; God's aim "is for depth of satisfaction" (*PR* 105).

This ideal goal for human life centrally involves the interplay of conscious and unconscious dimensions of experience. Jung and Whitehead both present a path to salvation—especially salvation from the false view of humans and our place in the universe promoted by modernity. And for both of them this salvation involves the integration of consciousness and the unconscious. It involves, that is, becoming conscious of dimensions of experience of which we are normally at most only dimly conscious (at least as modernity has defined and shaped "normal" experience). For Jung this task is at the center of psychotherapy. Whitehead makes this task of becoming aware of the unconscious dimensions of experience central for philosophy: "Philosophy is the self-correction by consciousness of its own initial excess of subjectivity." Its task, he says, is to "recover the totality" which is obscured by the selectivity of consciousness (*PR* 15). The difference within similarity here is at the heart of the complementary nature of archetypal psychology and process theology, making it possible for each to be enriched by the other.

Thus far, in arguing for the complementary nature of these two movements, I have pointed to their similarities. Their differences, however, are equally important.

III. Important Differences
between Whitehead and Jung

Many of the differences between the two thinkers are pointed to by the various essays in this volume. To summarize some of them: Whitehead's approach is avowedly philosophical, even metaphysical; Jung contrasts his empirical approach with philosophy, and disdains metaphysics. Whitehead sought to return to pre-Kantian modes of thought, circumventing the Kantian critique by correcting some errors in pre-Kantian philosophy (PR xi–xii); Jung's primary philosophical sources are Kant himself and post-Kantian philosophers, especially Schopenhauer and Nietzsche. Whitehead deals primarily with concepts, Jung with images. Whitehead is concerned primarily with cosmology, only secondarily with the human soul as a completion of the cosmology; Jung is concerned primarily with the soul, only incidentally with cosmology as the context of the soul. Whitehead employs the impersonal criteria of self-consistency and adequacy to the widest possible range of evidence, seeking to overcome personal bias and limitations of experience; Jung bases his thought largely on his own inner experiences.

Whereas I claim that these differences, or at least some of them, make the Jungian and Whiteheadian movements complementary, so that each can benefit from the other, a more pessimistic conclusion could be drawn—namely, that these differences, or at least some of them, are so profound as to forestall any attempt to pull Jungian and Whiteheadian thought together into a richer synthesis. This claim could be made, for example, if the contrast between images and concepts were raised to an outright opposition, which it has seemed to be in some of Hillman's writings (I deal with this issue in my essay in response to Hillman). Or this claim could be made in terms of the different philosophical traditions. The trajectory in which Jung stood—Kant, Schopenhauer, Nietzsche, Freud—has led, after all, to the aforementioned deconstructive postmodernism, in which the attempt to develop a worldview is given up in principle. This type of thought suggests that the determination of all perception and thought by preconscious factors—such as sex, race, socioeconomic class, culturally conditioned linguistic structures, and individual psychodynamic development—is so complete that all putatively "objective" criteria for adjudicating between worldviews are circular. The standard empirical criterion of adequacy to the facts, for example, cannot be applied, because all "facts" are socially and personally constructed, so that one person's "facts" will be another person's "illusion" or "ideology." Even the criterion of self-consistency can be regarded as a manifestation of the will-to-power rather than as an objective criterion of credible thought. Charles Winquist suggests in his essay herein that this deconstructive outworking of the post-Kantian tradition in which the archetypal movement arose prevents any union between it and the Whiteheadian movement, which remains optimistic about the process of constructing worldviews that progressively correspond more and more to the nature of reality itself.

My own position, to be partly presupposed and partly argued in the following section, is that, although the historic differences between the two movements are indeed profound, they are not finally insuperable. My belief is that those elements in Jung's thought that at first glance make his thought seem incompatible with that of Whitehead are not essential to his main insights. In fact, I believe, his main insights are undermined by those elements, and need something like Whitehead's cosmology for support. Before I argue this point, however, I make some suggestions for the reverse side of the complementarity: what process thinkers can learn from archetypalists.

IV. What Process Theologians
Can Acquire from Archetypal Psychology

The Jungian movement provides things that are not supplied to process theology by Whitehead. Chief among these is an empirical psychology. Whitehead provides only a philosophical psychology—a description of generic features of the human soul meant to be true of human beings always and everywhere. Although his position entails that the actual content of experience, as distinct from its formal structure, can only be known empirically, he does not do this empirical work, which would, of course, be the far more difficult task.

One could well reply, of course: Granted that Whiteheadians need to look somewhere for a viable empirical psychology, why should they look to Jung? Two answers: First, as I have already indicated, Jung's position on most general issues is very close to that of Whitehead. Second, and to be stressed because it has been so little noticed: *If Whitehead's philosophical position about nonsensory perception of the past is correct, then something like Jung's "collective unconscious," with its "archetypes," is what should be expected.* Assuming that this point, which I explain in section VII, is valid, followers of Whitehead's basic principles should be intensely interested in the results of the empirical research into the actual content of these archetypal forms that occupied so much of Jung's long life, a research that has been continued by many others in the Jungian movement, most notably by James Hillman.

A second respect in which those in the process tradition can be strengthened by the archetypal tradition involves the distinction between images and concepts. Clear conceptual thinking is extremely important, and Whitehead's philosophy encourages a high degree of conceptual clarity with regard to important issues. But most people, perhaps even philosophers, are moved more by images than by concepts. The White-headian movement has been notably less successful than the Jungian movement in *communicating* its vision to more than a tiny percentage of the populace. Whitehead pointed out that "it is more important that a proposition be interesting than that it be true"—because unless it is interesting, thereby becoming a "lure for feeling," no one will care whether it is true (*PR* 259; *AI* 244). But we Whiteheadians have for the most part been more concerned that our assertions be true than that they be interesting. Although we may have rationalized our ineffective-ness by telling ourselves that we were casting pearls before swine, we were actually—to use another New Testament image—giving hungry people stones, in the form of indigestible concepts.

The reason why these concepts are indigestible by most people, even if they are hungering and thirsting after a right vision, may be illuminated by a test of personality types based upon Jungian thought. The Meyers-Briggs test distinguishes between thinking types, feeling types, sensation types, and intuitive types, and evidently only about 10 percent of the population is comprised of thinking types. A movement that communicates primarily in terms of concepts instead of images is therefore destined to remain very much a minority movement.

This point about rhetoric implies a deeper point, one about the nature of human experience itself. The claim of the archetypal tradition is that the soul is essentially an imagining, symbolizing process, and that we function much more basically in terms of symbolic images than we do in terms of (allegedly) literal concepts. If this is true—and White-headian thought itself provides some reason to think it is—then all people, even those in whom conceptual functioning is highly developed, will be moved more fundamentally by images than by concepts. Ac-cordingly, process theologians may gain from archetypal psychologists a more accurate understanding of the nature of human beings as well as (and thereby) a more effective rhetoric.

Yet another thing Whiteheadians can derive from archetypalists is a *psychology* of creativity to flesh out our *philosophy* of creativity. This psychology of creativity contains, as well, advice on how to release our creativity, which could help Whiteheadians more fully unite theory and practice.

These four possibilities—an empirical psychology that is compatible with process theology, a more realistic understanding of human experience, a more effective rhetoric, and a psychology of creativity—should be sufficient to motivate process theologians to explore the archetypal tradition, in spite of the forbidding size of its corpus, the need to learn an esoteric language, and the difficulty of entering a developing movement so many decades after its origination.

I turn now to the complementary question: Why should archetypalists be sufficiently motivated to learn process theology, given these same daunting factors? My suggestion is that archetypal psychologists could acquire from process theology a philosophical-theological framework that is compatible with scientific evidence and the facts of ordinary experience as well as with the somewhat extraordinary dimensions of experience presupposed and focused on by archetypal psychology.

This discussion must be much more lengthy than the previous discussion of what process theologians can learn from archetypalists. Even though the values process theologians could acquire from archetypalists are hard to come by, requiring much time and effort, the discussion of them could be quite brief. The values offered by process thought in return have the opposite character: they could be appropriated rather easily, once it is seen that this appropriation would be desirable, but the discussion of this desirability involves complex, interrelated issues, and accordingly must be quite lengthy. One reason the issues in this direction are so much more complex is that, whereas Whitehead did not have an empirical psychology that might compete with Jung's, *Jung did have a philosophical position—including a speculative worldview as well as an epistemology*[9]*—that conflicts in some respects with that of Whitehead.* And Jung thought that this philosophical outlook was of a piece with his psychology. It takes considerable sorting out to see that Jung's psychological insights not only do not require his own philosophical position, but in fact require a philosophy more like Whitehead's for support.

This discussion occupies sections V–IX, with the following points discussed in order: (V) With its doctrine of panexperientialism and nonsensory perception, process theology provides the type of position on the *mind-body relation* required by archetypal psychology. (VI) This position in turn shows how *parapsychological phenomena*, which were so central to Jung's thinking, and even *life after death*, which Jung came to accept, are compatible with the facts of science and everyday experience. (VII) This position also provides a way of understanding how *archetypes* are inherited. (VIII) Process theology's pan-en-theism provides an alternative both to traditional theism, rightly rejected by Jung, and to Jung's own decision to locate evil in God—an alternative that is more consistent with Jung's own therapeutic and ethical concerns. (IX) Process theology's methodology reconciles Jung's desire to be empirical with his desire for a meaningful worldview, and is consistent with Jung's practice and many of his own methodological statements.

It is in these five sections, incidentally, that I function most explicitly as a process theologian, and in which this introduction goes beyond the usual bounds of an introduction, in approach as well as length, becoming an argumentative essay in its own right. In spite of its unusual nature, this argumentative portion is necessary to support the thesis of complementarity between the two movements, and also to prepare the way for understanding the extent of Hillman's departure from Jung's own program, by bringing out a range of issues from which Hillman means to prescind. Although in *form* this portion consists largely of a sustained argument against some of Jung's philosophical and theological ideas, its *intention* is to defend Jung's psychological ideas by showing that they are not necessarily tied to a worldview that is widely and rightly considered to be objectionable on rational, religious, and moral (including feminist) grounds. The purpose, in other words, is to remove unnecessary obstacles to a wider appropriation of Jung's central insights, which are invaluable, within religious, university, and morally activistic communities.

V. Nonsensory Perception
and the Mind-Body Relation

The mind-body relation can well be said to be the chief theoretical problem of modern thought. The modern decision to deny all interiority, experience, intrinsic value, and purpose to matter gave modern thinkers a dilemma with regard to the reality of our own experience, generally called our mind, psyche, or soul. On the one hand, one could say that the mind, with its experience, freedom, purposiveness, and intrinsic value, is different in kind from matter. But this creates the notorious mind-body problem: how could two wholly unlike things interact? For example, how could that which is impenetrable affect or be affected by that which does not occupy space in an impenetrable way? How could that which operates by final causation, or self-determination, interact with that which operates strictly by mechanistic efficient causation? How could that which is devoid of all intrinsic values have anything to share with that which is constituted by values? Early modern thinkers, such as Descartes and Malebranche, answered this question by appealing to a supernatural God, for whom all things are possible. But more recent dualists who cannot accept this supernatural solution have to plead ignorance. And other problems arise as well. For example, where does one draw the absolute line between experiencing and nonexperiencing beings: below the human mind, as did Descartes? below animals with a central nervous system? below life? If the latter, where does one draw the line between living and nonliving things? Any such line seems arbitrary. And how does one explain, without a supernatural creator, how experiencing mind emerged out of nonexperiencing matter in the course of evolution?

On the other hand, one can seek to avoid these problems of dualism by affirming a materialistic position, according to which "mind" is simply a word for the functioning of the brain insofar as it generates experience. But this seemingly monistic doctrine still has the same problem: how can nonexperiencing matter, even if it is organized in something as complex as a brain, "generate" experience? And this "identist" position, according to which mind and brain are identical, raises even worse problems. If matter, including the "gray matter" of the brain, operates mechanically, being devoid of all capacity for self-determination, the implication is that human experience, including every conscious decision, is wholly determined by the molecular interactions of the body; and yet everyone, including the deterministic philosopher, presupposes in practice that he or she is partially free. Another paradoxical implication is that the deterministic philosopher's "rational" conclusion that determinism is true is not in reality, according to the theory of determinism, based on rational insight but on deterministic molecular interactions. Determinism, besides logically leading to a fatalistic, nihilistic view of life, is a philosophy that no one can consistently live by in practice. We must therefore assume that it is false.

Although most writers in the archetypal tradition deal primarily with psychological as distinct from philosophical issues, most of them seem to agree that a materialistic, deterministic philosophical position would be incompatible with archetypal psychology, because a modicum of freedom in the sense of self-determination is presupposed. But this leads some of them in the direction of dualism. An example is provided by K. M. Abenheimer in an essay entitled "The Ego as Subject" in a collection of essays entitled *The Reality of the Psyche*.[10] After saying that "what the ego is, and how it can be described, is unclear," he reaches the following conclusions. The energies of the psyche are "not energies in the sense of natural science," because the concept of energy involved is based on "internal subjective experience" and therefore "does not refer to the measurable objective reality." Furthermore, "the psychic subject does not belong to the objective reality either." To indicate the different orders of existence involved, Abenheimer refers to Sartre's distinction between "being for itself" and "being in itself." The ego, he continues, "is immaterial and not identical with the body." He knows that Gilbert Ryle has "tried to debunk the concept of the subject by calling it 'the ghost in the machine.'" But Abenheimer says, sanguinely, that psychologists are "undisturbed by this behavioristic debunking." He concludes with this twofold position:

> The ego as project is always more than and different from any actuality, be it that of the body or of anything else. Yet this does not mean that there exists no relationship between body and ego. The ego acts throughout the body, expresses itself in it, is affected by bodily states of health or illness.[11]

As can be seen, Abenheimer only restates the problem. Granted that mind and body affect each other, the question is: How do we conceive of them so as to make this patent fact intelligible? How could that which, in Sartre's language, exists "for itself" (has experience) exchange information with that which merely exists "in itself" (has no experience)? Assuming that a ghost cannot affect a machine, and vice versa, how can we remain "undisturbed" by Ryle's critique if indeed the relation of mind to body is implied to be analogous to that of a ghost in a machine?

Jung himself, at least in some passages, was not undisturbed by dualism. He saw the philosophical problem clearly, saying:

> Psyche cannot be totally different from matter, for how otherwise could it move matter? And matter cannot be alien to psyche, for how else could matter produce psyche? Psyche and matter exist in the same world, and each partakes of the other, otherwise any reciprocal action would be impossible. (*CW* 9/I:413)

His desire to avoid dualism is seen also in his description of psychic energy as "a psychic analogue of physical energy" (*MDR* 208–9). In his desire to have a *unus mundus,* or unified world, he suggested that "psyche and matter are two aspects of one and the same thing" (*CW* 8:418). His main suggestion as to what this might be was that the archetypes might be "psychoid," capable of manifesting in either material or psychical forms of existence (*CW* 8:436).

These suggestions by Jung as to how to solve the problem were made in passing here and there in his writings; they were never developed into a systematic position. He in fact was conscious of not having solved the problem. In his last major work, he wrote: "Though we know from experience that psychic properties are related to material ones, we are not in a position to say in what this relationship consists or how it is possible at all" (*CW* 14:765).

In the light of this fact, and the fact that Jung himself was more philosophical than most of his followers, it is no surprise that the archetypal tradition has possessed no generally accepted solution to the mind-body problem. C. A. Meier, for example, has reported himself "keen to find a way out of the idea that there is a causal relation between psyche and soma."[12] He prefers to think of the relation as "synchronistic" (which, I will suggest later, is an even more problematic idea). Michael Fordham wants not to think of the body "as something 'external' to or separate from the psyche" but to think of psyche and soma "as two ways of looking at the same thing."[13] But that would seem to move toward a form of identism, which would threaten the affirmation of psychic freedom (as well as the possibility, in which Jung at least believed, of some form of psychic life after death). The mind-body relation does seem to constitute a genuine problem within the Jung-based tradition.

The ideas that were so tentatively and unsystematically suggested by Jung as the basis for a solution have been developed in systematic form by Whitehead. He shows how dualism can be avoided, so that mind-body interaction is intelligible, while reductionistic materialism is also avoided, so that the degree of freedom we presuppose is also intelligible.

Creativity is Whitehead's word for that "same thing" which, in Jung's words, "psyche and matter are two aspects of." As a broader concept than the physicist's "energy" (*AI* 186; *MT* 168), creativity is that ultimate reality which is embodied in all actual things (as distinct from real but nonactual forms). It is embodied, therefore, in electrons, atoms, molecules, macromolecules, cells, and the psyches of humans and other multicelled animals. Explaining not only how it can give rise to both what we ordinarily call "mind" and "matter," but also how "psychic creativity" is analogous to "physical creativity," brings us to one of Whitehead's most distinctive ideas. This is the idea that each enduring individual, such as an electron, molecule, or psyche, is in reality a rapidly repeating *series* of momentary events, called "actual occasions." A synonym is "actual entities." The point is that the fully *actual* entities, which were traditionally called "substances," are not enduring substances at all, but momentary events or occasions. Another synonym is "occasions of experience." The full point, then, is that the fully actual things of the world are events—but not just any type of events. Rather, they are *unified* events, and what gives them unity is that they are *experiences*. The world is ultimately made up of, in the phrase of William James, drops of experience.

Now each drop or occasion of experience—and this is the essential point for our present discussion—exists in two modes. First it exists as a subject. In this mode it is in the present, and enjoys experience. But after its moment of subjectivity (which might last a tenth of a second for a human occasion of experience, a billionth of a second for a subatomic occasion of experience), it is in the past, and as such exists as an object. As an object it no longer enjoys experience; rather, it can now be experienced (perceived) by later subjects.

This account provides a nondualistic way of understanding the distinction between subjects (experiencing things) and objects (nonexperiencing things). Rather than thinking of an ontological distinction between two wholly different types of things—subjects that are always subjects, objects that are always objects—Whitehead presents a purely *temporal* distinction: objects are things that once were subjects; subjects are things that will soon be objects. For an example, take memory: you as present subject remember prior moments of your psyche. Those prior moments are no longer experiencing subjects, but are now objects of your present experience. The past moments are *active* in your present experience, to be sure; the term "object" does not connote inertness but only the condition of no longer experiencing and making decisions, which brings us to the next point.

This distinction between existing as a subject and as an object correlates with *two different modes of creativity.* While an actual occasion is coming into existence as a subject, its creativity is embodied in the guise of *receptivity and self-determination.* Whitehead's technical term is "concrescence," which means "becoming concrete." In this mode, the creative energy of the occasion receives the influences from the past into itself, then synthesizes these influences into a unified experience. The occasion of experience is largely determined by the influences entering into it from the past, but it is not wholly determined by them. It finally determines for itself just how to synthesize the given materials, thereby manifesting a degree of freedom. These two aspects of the concrescence—the receptivity and the self-determination—constitute the dipolar character of the soul in each moment (which was mentioned in section I, above). The reception of the past is the "physical" pole, whereas the self-determination is the "mental" pole. This distinction between "physical" and "mental" poles is not the same distinction as the distinction between "subjects" and "objects," which I am in the midst of explaining.

When the actual occasion's moment of subjectivity is over and it exists as an object rather than a subject, it still embodies creativity, but now in a new mode. Creativity is embodied in objects in the guise of *efficient causation,* which means the influence of one thing upon another. Objects by definition are objects for subjects, and thereby exert influence upon them. An object, along with all the other objects existing alongside it, exerts a creative influence upon the future, thereby evoking a new set of subjects into existence, and the creativity then swings back over to the mode of concrescence. Creativity, in other words, eternally oscillates between these two modes.

From this perspective we can validate Jung's sense that "psychic energy" must be analogous to "physical energy" while recognizing the truth in the position of Abenheimer and other dualists that the psychic energy we experience in ourselves is different from the measurable energy of the physicist. The reconciliation of these seemingly opposed viewpoints is effected by recognizing that we know our own reality from within, in its subjectivity, whereas we know the reality of all other things only from without, in their objectivity. And the energy of things is measurable, by definition, only when they exist as objects. "Memory" is the name we give to that peculiar relation we have to our own past. Although these past experiences now exist only as objects, we remember what they were in themselves, as subjects. A chimpanzee, most of us believe, has a similar relation to its own past. The Whiteheadian suggestion is that this relationship applies analogously all the way down. A cell would therefore have some slight memory of what it experienced a few seconds earlier, and an electron an even slighter memory, perhaps going back no longer than a millionth of a second. The difference between subjects and objects, and therefore between psychic and physical energy, in other words, is the difference between present and past, and being known from within and being known from without. The difference is not ontological, but merely temporal and epistemological.

But surely, one protests, there must be a greater difference between subjects and objects! We cannot believe that rocks have feelings! This is true, and points to the need for one more distinction. Whitehead distinguishes, as did Leibniz (who is, along with Plato, probably the most important predecessor that Jung and Whitehead have in common), between two ways in which enduring individuals can be organized. (Leibniz called enduring individuals "monads," but this term suggests his view that they were windowless, which provides a good reason for Whiteheadians and Jungians to avoid it.) Enduring individuals, such as molecules, can be organized either into compound individuals, or into nonindividualized societies. The molecules in a living cell are organized into a compound individual. This means that, out of the organization, a higher-level individual, the cell itself with its life and unified experience, emerges. The molecules in a rock, however, do not give rise to a higher-order series of experiences that would give the rock a unified experience. The only experience in the rock is that of the individual molecules (just as, analogously, the only experience in a crowd of people is that of the individual people, even though the close relationships give rise to dimensions and dynamics of experience that would not occur otherwise).

Organization into compound individuals is a pervasive feature of the world. Atoms, molecules, macromolecules (such as DNA), viruses, bacteria, living cells, animals, and perhaps the universe itself (more on this later), among other things, can all be considered compound individuals, each having a "mind" or "soul" making them more than the sum of their parts. This mind or soul of the whole is its regnant or dominant member (Leibniz had spoken of the mind as the "dominant monad"). Because it has more power than any of the other members of the compound individual, the soul gives the whole organism a capacity to make a unified response to its environment. A soul or *anima* is a self-moving thing; the ordinary distinction between plants and animals reflects this point: animals can move around in ways that plants cannot.

This distinction between compound individuals and nonindividualized societies provides, from a Whiteheadian perspective, the basis for the most common distinction between mind and matter. We attribute mind or soul to self-moving things, whereas things considered mere matter are nonliving things with no capacity for self-movement (with nonindividualized but living things [plants] being somewhere between). We rightly suspect, generalizing from our own experience, that self-movement betokens experience, and where we see no evidence of a capacity for self-movement we refuse to speak of experience, mind, or soul. We will not, therefore, attribute experience or soul to sticks and stones, typewriters and (to give a more controverted example) computers. And we are right not to do so, says Whitehead. These things are purely material. And yet this does not mean an ontological dualism that would give rise to a mind-body problem, or to a problem of how mind could have emerged in the evolutionary process out of mindless matter. No *ontological dualism* is posited, only an *organizational duality.* The molecules, atoms, and even subatomic particles out of which the rocks and typewriters are made are not themselves wholly devoid of experience. So, the rock has experience *in* it—the primitive animist was this far correct; but the *rock itself,* considered as a whole, has no experience over and above that of its molecular parts.

The resulting position can be called "panexperientialism" as long as it is remembered that the "pan" refers to all *individuals* (simple or compound), not all things whatsoever. Aggregates such as rocks are not thought to have experience. (This point is stressed because the most common way to dismiss this position, prevalent even among otherwise intelligent people capable of reading, is to accuse it of saying that "rocks have feelings.")

This panexperientialist position overcomes the mind-body problem. If the psyche is only different in degree from the cells comprising the brain (even if the difference in degree is vast—about three billion years of evolution worth), then the interaction between the brain and psyche is not unintelligible. The psyche influences the brain cells by sharing its feelings (including its intellectual feelings, ordinarily called "thoughts") with them. From the point of view of the brain cells, this is their (nonsensory) perception of the psyche. The brain cells then influence the psyche in return by sharing their (relatively lowly) experiences with it. From the point of view of the psyche, this is its (nonsensory) perception of the brain.

The nonsensory perception mentioned in the previous paragraph is called "prehension" by Whitehead. This prehension is the receptivity, mentioned earlier, with which every occasion of experience begins. Panexperientialism implies that every actual entity enjoys perception, in the sense of this nonsensory prehension. Sensory organs are not necessary, in other words, to perceive, in the sense of prehend. It is therefore not absurd to attribute a type of perception to things such as cells, and even molecules and electrons. They can perceive their environment, in the sense of "internally take account" of it. This position also implies that, even in organisms with sensory organs, such as ourselves, *sensory perception is a secondary, not the primary, form of perception.* I can see the tree in front of me only because my psyche prehends the data transmitted *via* the photons to my eye through my optic nerve to my brain. It is thus exactly backwards to argue that perception requires sensory organs; the truth must be that sensory organs can produce sense-perceptions only by virtue of nonsensory perception. Sensory perception is a very indirect, mediated form of perception: literally millions of events of nonsensory perception have occurred between the tree and my sensory perception of it. This mediated perception can work only because of unmediated perception, which is what prehension is: the direct appropriation of data from an object (an object that, it should be recalled, had previously been a subject, and thus has the kind of data—namely feelings—that a subject of experience can appropriate). This idea that all causal interaction is by means of nonsensory perception thus makes the mind-body relation intelligible.

This panexperientialist position, which is a pluralistic monism (there are lots of actual entities, but only one ontological type), also makes human freedom intelligible. In this it differs from materialistic monism. This panexperientialism makes the freedom we all presuppose intelligible in terms of these two points: (1) All genuine individuals have at least some iota of freedom, in the sense of self-determination. Although each moment of experience is conditioned by its entire past, it is not wholly determined thereby. Each experience, after receiving influences through its prehension of previous experiences, exercises some self-determining creativity, through which it selects one set of possibilities from a larger set. (2) Higher-grade, more evolved individuals have more freedom: cells more than molecules, psyches more than cells, human psyches more than chimpanzee psyches. That is, higher individuals have more, not less, power than lower-grade ones. Here Whitehead, like Jung, reverses the reductionism of modern thought. The human psyche, far from being a purely epiphenomenal by-product of the really real material particles, is the most powerful creature on the face of the earth, embodying more creativity than any other. This creative power is twofold: the power of self-determination, and then the power to exert efficient causation upon others. This position is thereby adequate to the fact that human beings, with their technology, have changed the face of the planet more drastically than any other creatures, and are now the planet's biggest threat.

Whiteheadian panexperientialism thereby provides the kind of non-dualistic position, a *unus mundus* that nevertheless affirms human freedom, desired by Jung.

VI. Parapsychological Phenomena

This panexperientialism, with its degrees of creative actualities and its nonsensory prehension as the primary form of perception, also provides a basis for understanding how the three major topics of parapsychological research—extrasensory perception, psychokinesis, and life after death, all of which Jung affirmed—are possible. This is an issue, admittedly, in which some archetypal psychologists are little interested. But archetypal psychology that has been "modernized" by deletion of the parapsychological element is, given the fundamental role such phenomena played in the genesis of Jung's theories,[14] an attempt to keep the fruit without the root. The other reason for showing why Whiteheadian panexperientialism can make sense of parapsychological events is simply that there is good evidence for them (which I can here only baldly assert).[15]

It might be thought that archetypal psychology needs no philosophical help with parapsychological phenomena because Jung himself supplied a perfectly acceptable explanation with his doctrine of "synchronicity." This theory, however, is probably the weakest element in Jung's speculations. And it is an element that will forever prevent Jungian psychology from being integrated with the rest of science—which was Jung's aspiration, and a commendable one.

By "synchronicity" Jung means a meaningful but noncausal relation between two events. To use this concept for what is usually called "extrasensory perception," which Jung does, means that the perceived event in no way causes the person's perception of it. But why did he hold that? Why did he not hold, instead, that the event *evokes* a nonsensory perception in the person's mind?

Jung's position here is based on his acceptance of Kant's epistemology. The two greatest philosophical influences on Jung, at least among modern philosophers, were surely Kant and Schopenhauer (with Nietzsche probably coming in third). Jung describes Schopenhauer as "the great find," but then says that he found in Kant's epistemology "an even greater illumination" (*MDR* 70). Now Kant, on the one hand, equated perception with sense-perception. And he, on the other hand, thought of causation as occurring regularly and deterministically between contiguous events. The phenomena called "parapsychological," however, notoriously do not occur in any regular, predictable way, and they occur between events that are not contiguous but are separated by space, or time, or both. From a Kantian perspective, then, in which causality is an all-or-none affair, such phenomena cannot be considered cases of causal influence.

Kant's epistemology provided another element in Jung's doctrine of synchronicity. Kant held the categories of space, time, and causality to be purely phenomenal categories: they applied only to things as constructed by the mind out of sensory perceptions. Space, time, and causality, in other words, apply, so far as we know, only to appearances; we cannot assume that they also apply to the real world, the things in themselves. In fact, Kant often suggested that we could assume that these categories do *not* apply to reality in itself, and Jung followed him in this assumption. Jung's Kantian position on this point is reflected, for example, in his statement that "there was nothing preposterous or world-shaking in the idea that there might be events which overstepped the limited categories of space, time, and causality" (*MDR* 100). It is also reflected in his exaggerated claim that the parapsychological experiments of J. B. Rhine "prove that the psyche at times functions outside of the spatio-temporal law of causality" (*MDR* 304). Jung adds that, to make sense of these experiments, "we must face the fact that our world, with its time, space and causality, relates to another order of things lying behind or beneath it, in which neither 'here and there' nor 'earlier and later' are of importance" (*MDR* 305).

Jung should have said, more hypothetically, that this Kantian doctrine provides one possible interpretation of the phenomena. But even had he said this, I maintain, a strong commitment to this interpretation would make it impossible to integrate an interpretation of these phenomena with any acceptable philosophy of science.[16] The idea that every event has causes is surely one of the fundamental principles of a scientific outlook. The idea that quantum physics has overturned this "principle of causality" is a distortion. All that quantum physics has overturned is the principle of causality understood as *complete determination* of the present by the past, and therefore as allowing complete predictability in principle. Quantum physics is sometimes also said to sanction a *reversal* of causality, so that causal connections can run backwards, with the present affecting the past. But, in the first place, this way of talking is proposed by most serious physicists only as a simple way of describing certain phenomena for operational purposes, not as an ontological assertion. In the second place, the times involved are extremely tiny fractions of a second. Even those who take backward causation literally within quantum interactions would not allow this idea to be generalized to mean that Jung might have influenced Plato. In the third place, the mere fact that some quantum physicists talk about backward causation does not mean that the idea is intelligible.

On the need for a causal explanation, Jung would, at least in his more Schopenhauerian moods, have agreed. Insofar as he presupposed Schopenhauer's worldview, Jung was not giving up the principle of causality altogether. Schopenhauer, while heavily Kantian, believed in an underlying, blind Will, which is outside space and time and of which all individuals are phenomenal manifestations. This underlying Will causes two events in different places, or different times, that have a meaningful relation to each other. Although no causality is exerted by one event on the other, there *is* a causal explanation in the sense that each event had the same underlying cause.[17]

Insofar as Jung accepted this interpretation—and it does seem to have been his dominant one—his view is similar to that of Descartes's successor Malebranche with regard to causation between mind and matter. As a Cartesian dualist, Malebranche saw that there could be no direct interaction between mind and body. He therefore suggested that God causes the appearance of interaction: when my hand on the hot stove begins to burn, God causes me to feel pain and therefore to want to move my hand. Of course, I cannot move my hand, because the mind cannot affect the body, so God then obligingly moves my hand. This view, for obvious reasons, did not catch on with the scientific community. There is no reason to think that Jung's Schopenhauerian interpretation of synchronicity, which is essentially the same, will fare any better. At least not if there is a better interpretation of the phenomena. (I am assuming, against late modern thought, that the problem of interpretation cannot be avoided by simply denying or ignoring the phenomena.)

Whitehead's panexperientialism provides a framework in which these phenomena and those of ordinary science and experience can be accommodated. I begin with *extrasensory perception,* taken to mean *awareness,* conscious or unconscious, *of information that did not come to the person through sensory channels,* that is, that was not mediated to the psyche by the body. From Whitehead's point of view, the only thing extraordinary about extrasensory perception, as usually understood (that is, as *conscious* awareness of such information), is that the information in question has risen to consciousness. By hypothesis one is perceiving, at the level of nonsensory prehension, the entire environment all the time. The basic description of creativity as concrescence begins, "The many become one" (*PR* 21), and the "many" are comprised of *all* past events, not just those in the immediate (contiguous) past. Each event begins, in other words, by receiving into itself, by means of innumerable prehensions, influences from the past world, both immediate and remote. The immediately past world impresses itself with special force upon the perceiver so that it is normally prehended with more intensity. It is therefore more likely to evoke a conscious perception. But the remote past is also directly prehended, although generally much more weakly. Because of this lesser intensity, these prehensions of noncontiguous events generally do not rise to consciousness. But there is no reason in principle why they cannot. In fact, memory of one's own remote past is a form of conscious prehension of the remote past that is considered normal. What is usually called "extrasensory perception," then, is unusual not because it involves nonsensory perception, but only because the data of this perception have risen to consciousness.

Given this interpretation, extrasensory perception does not violate the normal principle of causality, which is that all events have efficient causes (which does not necessarily mean that the efficient causes completely determine them), and that efficient causation is exerted from the past to the present. To say that B prehends A is simply the reverse side of saying that A exerts causal influence upon B. And prehension is always of *antecedent* events, because only those events that have already completed their subjective process of concrescence provide anything concrete and objective to be prehended. An event cannot prehend its contemporaries, meaning events that are concrescing at the same time. (There is, it is true, no reason to think that causal efficacy at this level is limited to the speed of light: light is transmitted through a contiguous chain of events, while in nonsensory perception there can be an immediate prehension of influences from a remote event. So, extrasensory perception can be of "contemporary" events *if* "contemporary" is defined in the broad, Einsteinian sense of all those events that can neither influence nor be influenced by the percipient event by means of radiation. But in the stricter sense of "contemporary" being employed here, contemporaries cannot interact. This is no great restriction. Although the objects prehended are always in the past of the prehender, the time involved might be only a millionth of a second and thus be practically undetectable.) An occasion of experience also cannot prehend future events, because there are no such events to be prehended. Some future events may be largely settled in their basic contours by the trajectory of events in the past and present. But the principle that each event is partially self-determining in the moment means that no events are fully determined until they determine themselves at the time. The future does not somehow already exist, say "eternally" or "in the mind of God," so that it could in principle be perceived. The past is fully settled, but the future is still to be settled. It is partly indeterminate even for omniscience. To be omniscient is to know everything knowable, and the future is not knowable, at least in its details, because the future events do not exist. This principle, of course, stands in tension with the notion of "precognition," to which I will come shortly.

Although this interpretation differs from Jung's notion of synchronicity as a noncausal connection, it is consistent with some of his other statements. (Jung here, as on most topics, said various things over his long career.) After endorsing Kant's notion that the conscious mind "has only sense perceptions available to it" (*MDR* 316), Jung says: "I have never been inclined to think that our senses were capable of perceiving all forms of being" (*MDR* 351). This statement suggests that we have a nonsensory form of perception by which these other forms of being can be perceived. And, in the light of the fact that we sometimes become aware of these perceptions, the Kantian dictum that the conscious mind has only sensory perceptions available to it is contradicted. Jung also implies that objects other than sensory objects exert causal influence upon us. Although he in general accepted the Kantian notion that causality is a category applying only to the phenomenal realm based on sensory perception, so that the noumenal realm would be devoid of causality as well as space and time, he often, like Kant himself, suggests that the noumenal thing-in-itself exerts causal influence. For example, after enunciating the Kantian, solipsistic idea that we can perceive only our own psyche and its products, not things in themselves, he adds: "We have good reason to suppose that behind this veil there exists the uncomprehended absolute object which affects and influences us" (*MDR* 352). By Jung's own statement, then, parapsychological phenomena should not be interpreted as acausal in every sense. They are acausal only if "causality" is limited to contiguous events. But there is no good reason to define causation in this limited way. We should say instead that anything we perceive, however vaguely and unconsciously, exerts causal influence upon us.

In this way, extrasensory perception can be brought under an interpretive framework that does not violate the categories used for ordinary life and science. The only adjustment necessary is to broaden "causality" so that it includes every degree of causal influence, not just deterministic forms, and nonlocal (noncontiguous) causal influence as well as local. And this is hardly revolutionary: thanks largely to quantum physics, this broadening of the scientific and philosophical notion of causality has already occurred.

The second major form of parapsychological phenomena is psychokinesis. It was central in Jung's life. Several incidents are mentioned in his autobiography: the table splitting, the steel knife breaking, and the famous bookcase event involving Freud (*MDR* 105–6, 155–56).

Jung also attended séances involving spiritualistic phenomena for two years, out of which his doctoral dissertation arose (*MDR* 106–7). And his controversial *Septem Sermones*, which Jung later disowned but which contains, in Heisig's words, "a first systematic outline of the fundamental vision that lay behind ideas not to appear in his published works for many years to come,"[18] was preceded by reports by members of his family of a ghost, blanket snatching, and doorbell ringing (*MDR* 189–91).

Although Jung himself sought to interpret such phenomena as further examples of synchronicity, they can be interpreted better in terms of process theology's panexperientialism. I have already pointed out that, if prehension is the reverse side of causal influence, then causal influence acts at a distance as well as upon contiguous events. This causal influence at a distance is normally very weak compared with contiguous causation, and is generally undetectable, or at least undetected. We can define psychokinesis as any direct causal influence (unmediated by the body) of the psyche upon events outside the body. Parallel to the distinction between conscious and unconscious extrasensory perception, then, would be a distinction between *conspicuous* and *inconspicuous* psychokinesis. Influencing the behavior of bacteria, or moving a match or bending a spoon, without use of the body may simply be extreme, and therefore conspicuous, instances of a kind of direct influence of the psyche on the outer world that is going on more or less subtly all the time.

Whereas dualistic philosophies have generally had much more difficulty with psychokinesis than with extrasensory perception, panexperientialism can interpret both types of phenomena in terms of the same principles. What is psychokinesis from the point of view of the psyche would be nonsensory perception from the point of view of the moved object. This "object," according to panexperientialism, would be, in itself, a subject, or an aggregate of subjects. A bacterium, say, or the molecules in the matchstick or spoon, would prehend the human psyche, thereby incorporating influences from it. Panexperientialism thereby proves its ability, generally appreciated in scientific circles, to interpret seemingly disparate phenomena in terms of one set of principles.

It is important to note that, just as sensory perception is a very indirect process which presupposes nonsensory prehension, bodily action is a very indirect process which presupposes the direct causal influence of one thing upon another, beginning with the direct causal influence of the psyche upon the brain cells. Some philosophers of parapsychology, in fact, have defined psychokinesis as any direct action of the psyche upon something beyond itself, so that the influence of the psyche upon its brain would be an example. This would mean that, just as sensory perception involves nonsensory perception, bodily activity (such as bending a spoon with one's hands) presupposes psychokinesis. This is a dramatic way of making an important point, but I have preferred to employ the more standard definition of psychokinesis as the direct influence of the psyche upon things *outside* the person's own body. The point stands, however, that our bodily action upon the exterior world presupposes a more fundamental type of causal action, in which the psyche directly influences its body, and that this more fundamental causal action is parallel to psychokinesis. The only difference between the two is that the brain cells are contiguous with the psyche, whereas psychokinesis involves direct influence upon noncontiguous things.

One additional principle of the panexperientialist position that must be made explicit for understanding psychokinesis is the principle that the power of efficient causation is correlative to the power of freedom. Each occasion of experience, it will be recalled, embodies creativity. Higher-level experiences embody more creativity. Our own "psychic energy," as Jung called it, is evidently the highest embodiment of creativity on our planet. This creativity is, in the first place, the power to receive into ourselves more influence from the environment than can any other creature, and then the power to synthesize this variety of data into a unified experience, involving almost infinitely complex symbolic, imaginative, conceptual, affective, and volitional processes, both conscious and (mainly) unconscious. But then the creativity becomes, in the second place, the power to influence the subsequent environment in terms of the complex experience achieved. If our power to synthesize is greater than that of any other creature, then it follows that our power to exert causal influence upon the environment, both indirectly (through our bodies) and directly (psychokinetically), should be greater too.

This principle explains why psychokinetic events, at least of the conspicuous sort, seem to be caused primarily by human beings, seldom if ever by other animals. So-called poltergeist phenomena (bedcover snatching, doorbell ringing, and the like) typically occur in the neighborhood of disturbed pubescent children, who evidently need a release for pent-up emotional energy.[19]

This interpretation of psychokinesis, which involves direct causal influence of the psyche upon the surrounding world, is offered in place of Jung's interpretation in terms of an acausal connection or a causal connection referred to an underlying Will. But, like the interpretation of extrasensory perception I offered, it stands in harmony with some of Jung's ideas. In fact, although it is only implicit in Whitehead's thought that the human psyche is the most powerful agent on earth, this principle is explicit in Jung (*CW* 11:787).

The one parapsychological phenomenon that might seem to resist interpretation in process terms is apparent precognition. I say *apparent* because the term "precognition" already implies a particular and disputable interpretation of the events in question, thereby begging the question. The term means "knowing in advance." If one *knows*, in the strong sense, that X is going to occur, then X necessarily must occur. The idea of precognition therefore implies that future events in some sense already exist to be known, or at least that these future events are already completely entailed by the present, which implies a deterministic notion of history. Process theology denies both of these views. How then does it handle the kinds of occurrences that have been generally interpreted as precognitive? The easy solution would be simply to ignore such occurrences, or to dismiss them as "coincidences." But the evidence for such occurrences is about as good as it is for those occurrences usually regarded as psychokinesis, telepathy, and clairvoyance. So, if these other occurrences are accepted, some interpretation of apparent precognition is also called for. But how is that possible within a framework that insists that process is fundamental, that the future is partly open, that causality runs only from past to present, and that perception is accordingly always of past events?

There are actually many ways compatible with process theology to explain occurrences that are generally regarded as instances of precognition. I will mention four. First, in some cases the person may have received some sensory clues at a subliminal level, then made an unconscious inference and formed it into an image. For example, a person might pick up subliminal clues that a particular structure is unsound, subconsciously infer that a collapse will occur, then have a dream about such a collapse before it actually occurs.

Second, when all sensory clues, even subliminal ones, can be ruled out, one can employ the same explanation except for postulating that the person got the original information through extrasensory perception.

The person might learn through unconscious clairvoyance that a ship has sprung a leak. This information would rise into consciousness through the same process of unconscious inference plus a dramatization, through which the person "sees" the ship sinking some time before anyone on board knew about the problem. The person in a sense "knew" the event in advance of its occurrence, but the perception on which the knowledge was based was perception of present (or, strictly speaking, immediately past) circumstances. No backward causation, or forward perception, is involved. (Furthermore, the "knowledge" involved is not knowledge in the strict sense, because something could happen to prevent the ship's sinking. For example, it might run aground, or be rescued by another ship.)

A third possibility is that unconscious knowledge might be acquired of other people's intentions, or conditions, through telepathy. For example, a woman has a dream that a male friend in a remote place attempts suicide a week before he actually does. This dream occurs, one learns later, even before the man had (consciously) contemplated suicide. The explanation is that the man had unconsciously harbored a death wish for some time, and that the woman picked up this information telepathically and became conscious of it through a dream even before the man had become aware of his own suicidal wishes. She did not perceive the future, and the future did not exert some causal influence into its past.

A fourth possible explanation of some apparently precognitive events depends upon accepting psychokinesis as a sometimes powerful force. In a so-called precognitive experience, what generally occurs is a vision, often in a dream, followed by an event that corresponds closely to the vision, so closely that some sort of causal connection between the two seems probable. To call the event "precognition" is to assume that the causal relation runs from the event back to the vision. But, because causation normally runs from the present to the future, not in reverse, the more natural assumption would seem to be that the vision brought about the event. This is, admittedly, an initially startling idea. But if it is more startling than the idea that the future can affect the present, or that time is ultimately unreal, this is only because it is a less familiar idea, not because it is more paradoxical. In fact, it is not paradoxical or counterintuitive at all, whereas any attempt to make sense of backward causation, or of time's being ultimately unreal, quickly runs into self-contradiction. One reason the psychokinetic interpretation of so-called precognitive phenomena is so startling to modern minds is that these minds have been taught to regard themselves as epiphenomenal, and certainly as incapable of directly causing any effects outside the body. (Most modern minds even have difficulty with psychosomatic illness and cures.) But I am presupposing the agreement that the human mind is actually the most powerful creature on earth, not the weakest, and that we have good reason for accepting psychokinesis. Another well-accepted idea among parapsychologists is that, if and when large-scale psychokinetic effects occur, they are more likely to be induced by unconscious thoughts and feelings than by conscious intention, as evidenced in so-called poltergeist cases: the disturbed people, usually children, who are responsible for the strange happenings are typically unconscious, or at most only barely conscious, of their responsibility.[20] Images occurring in dreams, then, would possibly have a power to evoke responses in others—whether in physical objects, animals, or other people—that the person could not duplicate in waking hours by conscious willing. Another reason for rejecting the psychokinetic interpretation of such phenomena is that we moderns are repelled by anything suggesting the possibility of "witchcraft," or "black magic." We particularly do not want to consider the idea that our thoughts, even unconscious ones, might be responsible for destructive events. We should not, however, reject an otherwise plausible interpretation (assuming that it is) on the ground that we would prefer it not to be so. Many unpleasant things are true. In any case, this psychokinetic interpretation, which has in fact been offered by some of the most astute students of parapsychological phenomena,[21] provides a fourth possible interpretation that is fully in accord with process theology's basic principles.

The existence of these four possible interpretations (and there are more), all consistent with the ultimate reality of temporal distinctions, shows how precipitous it was for Jung to say that parapsychological data "prove that the psyche at times functions outside of the spatio-temporal law of causality," at least if this law is interpreted to allow influence at a distance. The data would prove (or better, suggest) this only if other equally plausible interpretations were not conceivable, and I have suggested several alternative explanations that are *more* plausible, and that do not violate the notions of time and causality presupposed in science and everyday existence.

The same principles of panexperientialism used for interpreting extrasensory and psychokinetic phenomena can also account for the possibility of the psyche's survival of bodily death (as well as out-of-the-body experiences while still living). The most common objections to belief in such survival are: (a) the psyche is not the sort of thing that could live without a body, especially a brain; (b) even if it could survive in some sense, it would not be able to perceive anything; and (c) even if it could somehow survive and perceive, it would not be able to act, so that this kind of existence would be highly frustrating and therefore undesirable. (It should perhaps be added that the modern mind rejects belief in survival, and any attempt to provide rational or empirical considerations in its favor, for reasons that transcend these particular objections. The modern mind has been taught that concern with life after death is somehow unseemly, and that even to entertain its possibility publicly is evidence of intellectual unsophistication. To discuss it as perhaps literally true is to enter the disreputable realm of the "mystical," the "esoteric," the "occult." The topic, in short, is taboo for modernity, especially as incarnate in the modern university. Aside from referring to an essay in which I have treated some dimensions of this issue [see n. 15], however, I can only say that I am here presupposing a *postmodern* context for discussion.)

The denial of the possibility of the psyche's survival is usually based on the assumption that the mind or psyche is somehow identical with the physical brain or an epiphenomenal by-product thereof, or at least that psyches are less fundamental in the nature of things than purely physical things, so that, although physical things can exist without experiences, experiences cannot exist without a physical base. All of these assumptions are rejected by panexperientialism, according to which nothing is more basic than experience itself. If the most primitive things in our universe, such as electrons or perhaps quarks, are nothing but series of experiences, then experience is self-supporting—that is, experience feeds off other experiences. It is true, of course, that *higher-level* experiences in compound individuals depend upon a complex organization of lower-level experiences: the life of the cell depends upon its molecular base, and the psyche of the squirrel depends upon its cellular base. But it may be that, although the psyche could never have *emerged* apart from a brain, a type of psyche might become powerful enough to *survive* apart from the particular kind of environment that was originally necessary to bring it into existence. Somewhere in its evolutionary development, in other words, the human soul might have acquired sufficient creative energy to exist apart from the brain. That great increase in power required for the development of the distinctively human capacity to generate symbols, as manifested both in dreams and in verbal language, may have simultaneously involved the power to survive apart from the physical body. The power to ask the question "When I die, will I live again?" may have been, simultaneously, the power to do so. No additional principle, such as supernatural intervention, is therefore necessary to conceive the possibility of survival.

The second question is whether a psyche, if it could survive, could also perceive. Some interpretations of extrasensory perception do not help in this regard, insofar as they regard it as a "sixth sense" or in some other way as a higher evolutionary development. But the idea that (conscious) extrasensory perception is rooted in a (normally unconscious) nonsensory perception that is more primordial than sensory perception provides a basis for thinking that the psyche, if it should find itself existing apart from its physical body, might still be able to perceive other things. These other things would then provide the soul with the nourishment it needs from beyond itself. Living apart from the brain would therefore not mean becoming a Cartesian substance that "requires nothing but itself in order to exist." It would only mean having overcome its dependence upon one particular type of environment.

The third question is whether the soul, granting that it could survive and perceive apart from a physical body, would be able to act. Without a voice box, hands, and sexual organs, would it be able to communicate meaningfully with others? (I leave aside here the possibility of an "astral," "ethereal," or "spiritual" body that might be virtually a double of our present body.) The idea that our primary kind of action upon others is direct influence, and that our bodily action is a secondary form of action, presupposing this more direct action, makes an affirmative answer to this question seem less inconceivable. Also, if all other things are perceivers, or prehenders, which would be able to prehend the psyche, and if prehension is simply the reverse side of causal influence, then the answer to the previous question has already supplied the answer to this one. The psyche would be able to act upon others insofar as those others are able to prehend its actions. Life after death would not need to be an existence of perpetual frustration.

Many archetypal psychologists (as well as many process theologians) are not much interested in this question of life after death, at least professionally. And indeed, it is much more of an optional element within Jung's own system than extrasensory perception and psychokinesis. But this does not make it unimportant. It is fundamental to archetypal psychology that the world is "a vale of soul-making"—that the very meaning and purpose of life is to develop the psyche. This process of soul-making will seem more important to most people if they believe that this process does not come to an abrupt end with bodily death but that their present life is part of a continuing journey.

This notion that life after bodily death might be a "continuing journey" presupposes, in accord with process theology, that time and process are fundamental in the nature of things, so that any life after death would also be a temporal life, with a distinction between a determined past, a self-determining present, and a partially-to-be-determined future. Jung's Kantian principles implied that any such life of the psyche apart from its sensory apparatus would be a timeless one: "the life of the psyche requires no space and no time" (MDR 319). And yet Jung commonly spoke of such a life in temporal terms. He said, for example: "It seems probable to me that in the hereafter, too, there exist certain limitations, but that the souls of the dead only *gradually* find out where the limits of the liberated state lie" (MDR 321; italics added). The idea that an extra-bodily psychic existence would still be temporal is, therefore, in opposition only to Jung's inconsistently held Kantian principles, not to his deeper convictions.

VII. The Inheritance of Archetypes

The notion of archetypes is, as the growing use of the term "archetypal psychology" implies, at the very heart of Jung-based theory. And yet the question of exactly how archetypes are to be understood is surrounded by controversy. One of the main questions, and the one to be explored here, is how archetypes come to be in the individual's psyche. If they indeed constitute a "collective unconscious" in which we all share, why is this so? As Andrew Samuels points out, Jung says that they are "inherited" but he was never clear about how.[22] Or, perhaps one should say, the clarity Jung reached in some moments was inconsistent with the clarity he reached in other moments. Sometimes he was Platonic, seeming to attribute causal power directly to archetypes as formal causes. At other times he regarded the archetypes as rooted in a cosmic principle—a Schopenhauerian blind Will, a Pleroma—which impressed them upon our psyches, or of which our psyches are simply individual manifestations. At still other times he suggested that innumerable repetitions of typical forms of experience had resulted in the archetypes being somehow present in the structure of our brains. And at still other times he seemed to suggest that the unconscious dimension of the psyche, understood to be distinct from the brain, somehow directly inherited the archetypes from those events in the past in which a typical form of behavior or experience was repeated innumerable times. Although process theology can accept a measure of truth in the second, third, and fourth of these explanations, it would have difficulty with the first.

Before proceeding with this discussion, I should point out a distinction, if only to dismiss it, between "archetypal images" and "archetypes in themselves," defined as utterly transcendent and unknowable (CW 8:417; 9/I:155; L/2:23). Whatever the full motive for this distinction, which was introduced by Jung only late in life, one of its effects was to admit the cultural conditionedness of the archetypal images while retaining the universality and virtual eternity of the archetypes *per se*, an issue to be discussed later.[23] I ignore this distinction (as do Hillman and some others in the Jungian tradition), because, if "archetypes in themselves" are utterly unknowable, we should not talk as if we knew something about them, even their existence.

One of the basic reasons some archetypal psychologists might have for considering process theology fundamentally incompatible is Whitehead's "ontological principle." According to this principle, only actualities can act. Therefore, "to search for a *reason* is to search for one or more actual entities" (PR 24). One negative implication of this principle is that formal causes, which are understood to be possibilities rather than actualities, cannot by themselves account for anything. Formal causes are discussed by Whitehead primarily in terms of "eternal objects," which he also calls "pure possibilities," and which are somewhat similar to Platonic forms. The force of the ontological principle is that these forms cannot act on their own; they can be effective only insofar as they are embodied in actual entities, which alone have the creative energy with which to act. Whitehead's ontological principle does not mean that he, any more than Jung, reduced all active causation to efficient causation from the past to the present, because he also defined it as the "principle of efficient, and final causation" (PR 24). In other words, besides the efficient causation exerted on the present by past actual entities, there is the self-determination or final causation exerted by the present actual entities on themselves, partly on the basis of their appetites for the future. But Whitehead's ontological principle, which is fundamental to all process theology, does rule out the idea of forms acting on their own, as distinct from being effective by virtue of being embodied in actual things, that is, in experiences. Any system of thought based upon that idea of formal causation would be incompatible with process theology.

Although Jung himself did sometimes write as if archetypes exerted causation directly upon the psyche, and some of his followers take these passages as definitive, his other accounts are all consistent with the ontological principle. This is true of those passages in which he roots them in an unconscious cosmic Will, and this notion seems to lie behind those passages in which the power of causal influence is apparently attributed to the archetypes themselves. That is, the latter passages reflect Jung's attempt to restrict himself to an "empirical" description of the data; the references to a cosmic Will, or Pleroma, represent the successful breakthrough of his speculative instincts. More Platonic statements, which seem to attribute causal efficacy to the archetypes themselves, should therefore, on this interpretation, not be taken as definitive of Jung's *philosophical* position. (I refer to this as a "Platonic" position, although Plato himself in some passages explained the efficacy of his Forms by seeing them as present within a cosmic Psyche.) However, regarding the archetypes as derived directly from a cosmic soul inevitably divinizes them, thereby making them all, even the most destructive ones, unchangeable and sacrosanct—a problem I discuss in section VIII.

The third and fourth interpretations, according to which the archetypes exist in us due to our inheritance of typical forms of experience that have been repeated innumerable times in the past, are also consistent with the ontological principle, because the efficient causation is attributed to those past experiences.

Jung makes statements suggesting one or the other of these latter two interpretations many times. For example, he says that "the collective unconscious, being the repository of man's experience . . . , is an image of the world which has taken eons to form" (*CW* 7:151). Jung says that the origin of the archetypes "can only be explained by assuming them to be deposits of the constantly repeated experiences of humanity" (*CW* 7:109). The archetypes are features of our image of the world that have "crystallized out in the course of time" because they "have been emphasized throughout the accumulation of similar experiences" (*CW* 7:151). Archetypes are "recurrent impressions made by subjective reactions," "impressions of ever-repeated typical experiences" (*CW* 7:109). Jung says elsewhere: "There are as many archetypes as there are typical situations in life. Endless repetition has engraved these experiences into our psychic constitution" (*CW* 9/I:99). Jung often refers to archetypes as "the history of mankind" written in our minds, but he sometimes goes beyond this, suggesting that animals too may have archetypes, and that our collective unconscious includes "residues of functions from man's animal ancestry" (*CW* 7:109, 159). He says that we can speak of "the psychology of the worm, and even of the amoeba" (*CW* 8:322).

This explanation, according to which the archetypes present in our unconscious experience are the effects of the activities of innumerable prior individuals, is consistent with the ontological principle that all causal effects must finally be attributed to individual actualities. Jung sometimes affirms this principle, saying that "even collective ideas once sprang from single individuals" (*CW* 11:269).

If this explanation is consistent with Jung's view that individuals are the locus of all value and power, why did he not use this explanation more consistently? And why has it not been the explanation emphasized by his followers? Part of the reason is surely that Jung was captivated—*the word is not too strong*—by Schopenhauer's vision of the world as a manifestation of a blind cosmic Will. But another important reason is surely that it has been difficult to understand how innumerable repetitions of a certain form of experience in the remote past could, by themselves, account for anything in the unconscious experience of present-day human beings. "What is the mechanism to explain this?" the modern mind immediately asks.

Some followers of Jung speak of a biological inheritance, whereas others speak specifically of a certain portion of the brain.[24] But such suggestions are appeals to mystery: we have no idea how such archetypes could be impressed upon the brain or otherwise transmitted biologically. Also, these suggestions imply a type of Lamarckian inheritance for which we have little evidence. (Jung's distinction between archetypes *per se* and archetypal images, and his insistence that only the former are inherited,[25] does not prevent an element of Lamarckian inheritance from being involved.) That by itself should not rule out the suggestion, but it at least should lead us to ask if the fourth interpretation, according to which archetypes are inherited directly by the psyche (as distinct from the brain), might not be possible.

Whitehead's process theology provides a basis for this fourth explanation. I did not realize this until Rupert Sheldrake's "hypothesis of morphic causation" led me to understand Whitehead's doctrine of prehension more fully. Sheldrake's basic hypothesis is that the more times a particular form is repeated, the more likely it is that a present member of the same species will repeat this form.[26] This hypothesis requires some kind of influence at a distance, especially temporal distance. Sheldrake uses the language of field theory, speaking of a "morphic field" that is created by repetitions of a given form. Whitehead's principles explain how such a "field" could be created.

The main point of this explanation is that a present event prehends a past event through many routes. The modern doctrine, according to which causation and perception occur only between contiguous events, would say that a particular remote event, let us call it A, would be perceived by the present event, let us call it P, only once, and only indirectly at that, that is, *via* event B (which came just after A), which is perceived indirectly *via* C, which is perceived indirectly *via* D, and so on, with all of them in the chain of contiguous events perceived indirectly except O, which occurs just before P, and which is alone perceived directly. But let us assume with Whitehead that we perceive (prehend) remote events directly, as well as indirectly *via* a chain of contiguous transmission. Then P would perceive A through many routes: directly, indirectly *via* B, indirectly *via* C (which would prehend A directly as well as indirectly *via* B), indirectly *via* D (which would have prehended A directly and also indirectly *via* C and B), and so on. The same would be true of P's prehension of B, and so on through C, D, E, et cetera. Now let us add the assumption that A, B, C, D, et cetera are fundamentally similar, with each event essentially repeating the form of its predecessor (while having some contingent content). This means that the form in question will be prehended by P—or, to put the point in causal language, will be impressed upon P—a large number of times. Because of this reinforcement induced by so many repetitions, this element in P's experience will be much stronger than forms that are perceived only once or a relatively small number of times. The form may, in fact, impress itself so strongly upon the unconscious of the perceiver as to have a "numinous" quality about it.

Whitehead's position, with its doctrines of perception and therefore causal influence at a distance, can in this way explain both Jungian archetypes and Sheldrake's morphic resonance. One advantage to archetypal theorists in accepting this explanation is that it would be based upon a philosophical position that is increasingly being regarded as adequate to a wide range of data—scientific, ethical, religious, and aesthetic. Also, to the degree that Sheldrake's hypothesis is accepted in the coming years, having an explanation that conforms well to his data and theory will provide archetypal psychology with the positive association with the physical sciences which Jung desired but which has thus far been elusive. Furthermore, this explanation through innumerable repetitions of typical experiences would free the notion of archetypes from those associations that have been most problematic, and have evoked the most criticism—from especially theological, ethical, and feminist points of view. This point will be explained in the next section, which deals with the central theological question of the nature of the divine.

VIII. The Divine Reality

The aspect of Jung's thought that has generated the most controversy is probably his discussion of God. Much of the controversy has involved simply trying to determine exactly what Jung meant by "God." Was he an atheist, a pantheist, an agnostic, a gnostic, or simply observing the methodological limitations of an empirical scientist? But much of the controversy has been generated by the fact that, whatever Jung meant by "God," he rejected the traditional picture of God as perfectly good, instead locating evil as well as good in God. I suggest in the following discussion that process theology, which also rejects traditional theism, provides another alternative for conceiving the divine reality which would provide a better theological base for archetypal psychologists. This alternative view, which retains the perfect goodness of God by denying the traditional doctrine of divine omnipotence, would retain the strengths of Jung's view—taking the reality of evil seriously, and helping us accept, rather than defensively refusing to acknowledge, the evil present in us—while overcoming its weaknesses—its tendency to give divine sanction to all archetypes indifferently, and to undermine the real distinction, which Jung did not deny, between good and evil in the world.

Jung's rejection of traditional theism, and the formulation of his own heterodox concept of God, evidently arose out of his struggles with the problem of evil. It may be, as has been suggested (see the quotation from Edward Whitmont in section IX), that his problematic relationship with his father, who was a theologian, was an important factor. But what seems most clear is that the Calvinistic notion of divine omnipotence, which Jung would have had impressed upon him at home as well as at church and from the Swiss culture in general, set the context. Although Jung was quite quickly able to give up the total goodness of God, the traditional association of God with overwhelming power was another matter. This deep-seated association, with its implications for God's relationship to evil, a dream that Jung considered a special revelation to him, his penchant for opposites, and the influence of Schopenhauer seem to have been the main ingredients in his own understanding of the divine.

Jung describes the decisive factors leading to his rejection of traditional theism in his autobiographical *Memories, Dreams, Reflections*. (It may be that we cannot take everything in this book, dictated by Jung in his eighties, as the way it really was; but what is important, in understanding the position of Jung in his mature years, is what in retrospect seemed decisive.) In this account Jung correctly pulls out the implications of the traditional doctrine of omnipotence (which the Calvinism dominant in Switzerland had accentuated). According to this doctrine, all power essentially belongs to God. The world, having been created *ex nihilo* through an entirely voluntary act of God, has absolutely no power of its own with which it could act contrary to the divine will. Any power possessed by creatures is on loan, as it were, and could be withdrawn or overridden at any time. Anything that happens in the world, therefore, must be in accord with God's will: either God caused it, or God permitted it while having had the power to prevent it. Jung, accordingly, in recounting his early reflections about God and sin, says:

> Adam and Eve . . . had no parents, but were created directly by God, who intentionally made them as they were. . . . God in His omniscience had arranged everything so that the first parents would have to sin. *Therefore it was God's intention that they should sin.* (*MDR* 38)

Jung recognized that this conclusion cannot be avoided by appealing to Satan. If the devil was created good, as orthodoxy said, then why the devil became evil was inexplicable (*MDR* 62–63). Besides, if the devil is a mere creature, as orthodoxy said, then it has no autonomous power: "The devil appeared to me no worse than a powerful man's vicious watchdog, chained up. Nobody had any responsibility for the world except God" (*MDR* 46).

The problem of evil was raised not only by human sin, but also by natural evil. "Certainly the world is immeasurably beautiful, but it is quite as horrible. . . . [I]f God is the highest good, why is the world, His creation, so imperfect, so corrupt, so pitiable?" (*MDR* 58). Jung says that the inability to find an answer to the problem of evil in the philosophers and theologians he studied ended his belief in traditional theism. In reference to Biedermann's *Christliche Dogmatik*, which Jung considered to be the best of the theological books he found in his father's library, he said: "What were the reasons for suffering, imperfection, and evil? I could find nothing. That finished it for me" (*MDR* 59).

This theoretical questioning was reinforced by, and surely inter-mixed with, a vision that Jung considered revelatory. Once while he was eleven years old, he had been thinking of the beauty of the world, and of the cathedral, and of God sitting above it all on a golden throne, when he had the sense that a terrible thought was about to come to him, one that would be a sin against the Holy Spirit, which would lead to his eternal damnation. He managed to hold back the thought for several days, until he became convinced that God wanted him to think the terrible thought. (The idea cited above, that it was God's intention that Adam and Eve sin, was the liberating thought.) So he let the thought come:

> I saw before me the cathedral, the blue sky. God sits on His golden throne, high above the world—and from under the throne an enor-mous turd falls upon the sparkling new roof, shatters it and breaks the walls of the cathedral asunder. (*MDR* 39)

This vision had a powerful effect upon the young Jung:

> I felt an enormous, an indescribable relief. Instead of the expected damnation, grace had come upon me, and with it an unutterable bliss such as I had never known. I wept for happiness and gratitude. The wisdom and goodness of God had been revealed to me now that I had yielded to His inexorable command. It was as though I had experi-enced an illumination. (*MDR* 40)

This illumination involved "the dim understanding that God could be something terrible." Jung says that this "dark and terrible secret" overshadowed his whole life (*MDR* 40). This secret was "that God wants to force me to do wrong . . . to experience His grace" (*MDR* 42). He now "knew from experience that God . . . wished to evoke not only man's bright and positive side but also his darkness and ungodliness" (*MDR* 70). He came to regard this event as a personal revelation from God: "He had even allowed me a glimpse into His own being. This was a great secret" (*MDR* 93). And he came to understand "the deepest meaning" of it to be that "God Himself had disavowed theology and the Church founded upon it" (*MDR* 93). Jung therefore knew from direct experience, indeed from a direct revelation, the same conclusion that followed from theoretical reflection upon worldly evil and divine omnipotence: God must be the source of all evil as well as of all good.

The notion of divine omnipotence was as important to Jung's revelation as it was to the theoretical reflection, as shown by his account of his state of mind leading up to the experience:

I could not yield before I understood what God's will was and what He intended. For I was now certain that He was the author of this desperate problem. . . . [F]rom the moment I emerged from the mist and became conscious of myself, the unity, the greatness, and the superhuman majesty of God began to haunt my imagination. Hence there was no question in my mind but that God Himself was arranging a decisive test for me. . . . In His omnipotence He could easily lift this compulsion from me, but evidently He is not going to. . . . (*MDR* 39)

Likewise, in his account of his reflections after the revelatory experience, he says, regarding his father:

But he did not know the immediate living God who stands, omnipotent and free, above His Bible and His Church, who calls upon man to partake of His freedom, and can force him to renounce his own views. . . . In His omnipotence He will see to it that nothing really evil comes of such tests of courage. (*MDR* 40)

With a different theological background, Jung's vision, had it occurred at all, might well have been given a quite different interpretation.

In any case, Jung's conclusion that God is the source of evil, or what is usually considered such, was reinforced by later reading. From Goethe's *Faust* he "found confirmation that there were or had been people who saw evil and its universal power, and—more important— the mysterious role it played in delivering man from darkness and suffering" (*MDR* 60). Then he came across Schopenhauer, whom he called "the great find." Schopenhauer confirmed Jung's suspicion that evil must somehow be present in the very root of the universe:

> He was the first to speak of the suffering of the world, . . . and of confusion, passion, evil. . . . Here at last was a philosopher who had the courage to see that all was not for the best in the fundaments of the universe. He spoke neither of the all-good and all-wise providence of a Creator, nor of the harmony of the cosmos, but stated bluntly that a fundamental flaw underlay the sorrowful course of human history and the cruelty of nature: the blindness of the world-creating Will. (*MDR* 69)

Jung says Schopenhauer's "somber picture of the world" had his "undivided approval." He does, to be sure, say that reading Kant led him to discover a fundamental flaw in Schopenhauer's system, "the deadly sin of hypostatizing a metaphysical assertion, and of endowing a mere noumenon, a *Ding an sich,* with special qualities" (*MDR* 70). This statement could imply that Jung rejected the notion of a blind, world-creating Will. But, as will be discussed in the following section, Jung's references to Kantian epistemology are generally more obfuscating than illuminating of his actual practice and beliefs, and this one is no exception. There is ample evidence—as was seen above in discussing "synchronicity" and will be seen further below—that the notion of an unconscious Will of cosmic scope was fundamental to Jung's thinking to the end. In spite of many statements that could be taken to indicate the contrary, he did not restrict "God" simply to the human collective conscious, which would have come into existence only with the emergence of human beings in the evolutionary process.[27]

Out of this combination of reflection, revelation, and reading came Jung's idea of the divine: a reality in which good and evil were equally present. He says, for example: "To believe that God is the Summum Bonum is impossible for a reflecting consciousness" (*CW* 11:662). Job's problem, he says, was that he "looked upon God as a moral being" (*CW* 11:586). The main theme of Jung's *Answer to Job* was "a picture of God's tragic contradictoriness" according to which "God is at odds with himself" (*MDR* 216; *CW* 11:567). Good and evil are, like all the other opposites, present in God. This conclusion follows, of course, if one accepts an essentially monistic, pantheistic view of reality, and Jung evidently did, saying of God: "He is everything in its totality, therefore, among other things, he is total justice, and also its total opposite" (*CW* 11:574). Jung could point to many ideas present in the Bible and traditional Christian doctrine, of course, to support his view. Against the Protestant theologian Friedrich Gogarten's view that "God can only be good," Jung quipped: "Yahweh could certainly have taught him a thing or two" (*CW* 9/II:80; 11:480). In his argument with Martin Buber, he said that the unconscious contains a "paradoxical God-image which will not square at all with the beauty, sublimity, and purity of the dogmatic concept of God. The God of Job and of the 89th Psalm is clearly a bit closer to reality, and his behaviour does not fit in badly with the God-image in the unconscious" (*CW* 18:1511).[28]

One way this revision of traditional theism came to expression was a doctrine of Divine Quaternity. Jung found the doctrine of the Trinity incomplete: its failure to include the principle of evil meant that a devil outside of God had to be posited (*CW* 11:103, 249). (Jung portrayed the fourth element in the Divine Quaternity alternatively as the evil principle, materiality, and the feminine principle [*CW* 11:125–26, 251–52], which is one of the features of his thought that has alienated feminists.) This inclusion of evil within God leads Jung to believe that his position alone is truly monotheistic, because a true monotheism, which roots everything in God, must assume that all opposites are contained in God (*CW* 11, p. 358). With this doctrine we circumvent the dualism introduce into Christian thought by Manicheanism, returning to the true monotheism according to which God rules the world with right and left hands (*CW* 11, pp. 357–58). Jung was in error historically to think that the major Christian theologians, such as Augustine, Thomas, Luther, Calvin, or Jung's fellow countryman Karl Barth, had given up this doctrine,[29] but his statement shows how thoroughly he retained the traditional doctrine of God's omnicausality. He differed from the traditional theologians only in concluding, correctly, that with such a doctrine one had to speak of God as evil as well as good— assuming the reality of genuinely evil events.

If Jung felt constrained to keep the traditional association between God and unqualified omnipotence, how could he overcome the association, which has been almost as powerful in Christian circles, between God and unqualified goodness? The answer is evidently Jung's view of God as an unconscious force rather than a conscious being. Having commented on the problem of evil created by the "naive assumption that the creator of the world is a conscious being," Jung says:

> Divine unconsciousness and lack of reflection . . . enable us to form
> a conception of God which puts his actions beyond moral judgment
> and allows no conflict to arise between goodness and beastliness. (*CW*
> 11:600n.13)

This doctrine of divine unconsciousness also helped, Jung believed, to explain the slowness and indirectness of evolution, which is simply one aspect of the problem of evil: Why would an omnipotent, consciously omniscient being use such a method to create the world? In opposition to the idea that "the Creator [is] conscious of Himself," Jung says that it is not probable "that the extremely indirect methods of creation, which squander millions of years upon the development of countless species and creatures, are the outcome of purposeful intention" (*MDR* 339).

Finally, this doctrine of the divine unconsciousness became the basis for an answer to Jung's search for something "which might confer meaning upon the banality of life" (*MDR* 165). He combined this doctrine of divine unconsciousness with the awareness that, apart from being consciously known, "no world exists" (he means the *phenomenal* world, the world as consciously known). The resulting conclusion is that, if human consciousness were to be extinguished, "the world would sink into nothingness." Schopenhauer's great achievement, Jung says, lay in recognizing this fact and thereby "the cosmogonic dignity of human consciousness" (*MDR* 279). This notion became the "explanatory myth" that satisfied Jung's need for "a view of the world which adequately explains the meaning of human existence in the cosmos" (*MDR* 338, 340). "That is the meaning of the divine service, of the service which man can render to God, . . . that the Creator may become conscious of His creation" (*MDR* 338). Jung's more complete statement shows how important it became to him to think of the creative power of the universe as unconscious:

> By virtue of his reflective faculties, man . . . demonstrates that nature
> has put a high premium precisely upon the development of conscious-
> ness. Through consciousness he takes possession of nature by recog-
> nizing the existence of the world and thus, as it were, confirming the
> Creator. The world becomes the phenomenal world, for without con-
> scious reflection it would not be. If the Creator were conscious of
> Himself, He would not need conscious creatures; . . . [Compared with
> the seemingly haphazard course of biological evolution] the history
> of the mind offers a different picture. Here the miracle of reflecting
> consciousness intervenes—the second cosmogony. The importance of

consciousness is so great that one cannot help suspecting the element of *meaning* to be concealed somewhere within all the monstrous, apparently senseless biological turmoil, and that the road to its manifestation was ultimately found on the level of warm-blooded vertebrates possessed of a differentiated brain—found as if by chance, unintended and unforeseen, and yet somehow sensed, felt and groped for out of some dark urge. (*MDR* 339)

This "dark urge" is none other, of course, than the "blind Will" of Schopenhauer, even if Jung did not accept every aspect of the latter's metaphysics.

We can see, therefore, that the idea of the divine as an omnipotent but unconscious force, in which good and evil along with all other opposites are combined, became the very key to Jung's worldview, explaining the problem of evil in general, the nature of evolution in particular, and the meaning of human life most particularly. The difficulty inherent in the idea that God is partly evil was dissolved by the thought that God is unconscious, and this latter thought provided a meaning for human existence. Jung would have been very unlikely, therefore, to have given up the idea of God as embodying evil: the very meaningfulness of his life had become bound up with it.

Jung had yet another major reason for becoming committed to the idea of God as embodying evil as well as good. The idea that God is wholly good, and hates evil unqualifiedly, Jung thought, makes it difficult for human beings to acknowledge the evil within themselves. By not consciously accepting it, they not only cannot be transformed but also tend to project their "shadow" onto others, and doing so becomes a major source of historical evil. The idea that God too embodies evil, Jung became convinced, was therefore not only true but also of great salvific importance, especially for overcoming the horrendous evils of modern existence.

Jung's idea of God is, nevertheless, problematic. One problem is that, because "God" is by definition that in which *is* and *ought* are identical, whatever God is like or wills is sanctioned as right. If one adds that God is omnipotent, and thereby the source of all happenings in the world, one thereby implies, with Alexander Pope, that "whatever is, is right." And Jung indeed says:

We must beware of thinking of good and evil as absolute opposites. . . . Recognition of the reality of evil necessarily relativizes the good, and the evil likewise, converting both into halves of a paradoxical whole. (*MDR* 329)

The implication seems to be that the evil is not genuinely evil from an ultimate standpoint (from a God's-eye view, if only God were conscious), because the evil is necessary for the good, and is in that sense good. Jung in fact says, in opposition to the idea that good and evil are metaphysical entities: "If we call everything that God does or allows good, then evil is good too, and 'good' becomes meaningless" (*CW* 9/II:423). And yet the very meaning of "God," at least if God is defined as omnipotent in the traditional sense, implies that everything that God does or allows must be considered good, so the conclusion that Jung means to be a *reductio ad absurdum* would follow: both "good" and "evil" would be meaningless.

And yet Jung did not hold, at least consistently, to the complete relativity of good and evil, in the sense that everything is equally good. He said: "The relativity of 'good' and 'evil' by no means signifies that these categories are invalid, or do not exist" (*MDR* 330). And one cannot read Jung's description of "Western man," as "greedy, violent in his pursuit of the goods of this world" (*CW* 11:772), and think that Jung thought the development of such a self was a good, or even a neutral, phenomenon. Writing with reference to the Nazism and Bolshevism of the time, he said:

> The Christian world is now truly confronted by the principle of evil, by naked injustice, tyranny, lies, slavery, and coercion of conscience. . . . In the face of that, evil can no longer be minimized by the euphemism of the *privatio boni*. Evil has become a determinant reality. (*MDR* 328–29)

These are not the words of a man who thinks that these things that ordinary mortals consider evil are really, from the perspective of a higher wisdom, matters of indifference. The divine turd in his dream may have smashed the walls that would have confined Jung's mind within his father's orthodox theology, but it did not completely obliterate the distinction between good and evil. Jung may have thought that the evil engulfing the world in the twentieth century was the result of a splitting of the divine wholeness, in which God as Satan was split off from God as Light (*MDR* 333–34). But Jung clearly did not think it a good thing that that splitting occurred, so he did not really accept the equal goodness of all developments. The first problem with Jung's idea of God, then, is that its way of solving the problem of evil implies a more complete relativization of the distinction between good and evil than even Jung, as much as he may have regarded himself to be an anti-moralist, could accept.

A second problem with his idea of the divine, closely related to the first, is that it provides a divine sanction for everything regarded as an archetype. Demaris Wehr, who is sympathetic with Jung on most issues, is one who has made this point. She has no interest in giving up the concept of the archetype, which she considers "the central Jungian concept," without which "the Jungian system loses its very foundation."[30] The problem arises from Jung's equation of the collective unconscious, from which the archetypes arise, with God, which means "placing . . . good and evil on the same level—ontologically, psychologically, and theologically."[31] The result is that Jung's psychology

> makes no real distinction between types of archetypal experiences. If an experience is "numinous," it is archetypal and in some way partakes of divinity. This elevation has the effect of cosmic endorsement.[32]

Having all archetypes come directly from the collective unconscious understood as the divine source of all things, in other words, prevents one from seeing some archetypes as *socially constructed.* Wehr's essay, contained in a book entitled *Feminist Archetypal Theory,* is concerned in particular with "Jung's and the Jungians' explanations of archetypes of the feminine and of the anima," which are "descriptively, and also prescriptively, limiting images of women in a partriarchal society."[33] They have this prescriptive, unchangeable character insofar as they are regarded as divinely revealed, as opposed to socially constructed in partriarchal societies. Whereas Jung meant for it to be freeing to see social-role definitions for women as archetypes of the feminine, Wehr claims that "precisely the opposite effect occurs." Because of the onto-theological status given all archetypes, "Jungian theory can function as quasi-religious or scientific legitimation of the status quo in society, reinforcing social roles, constricting growth, and limiting options for women."[34] This second problem is finally the same as the first: Jung's doctrine implies the equation of is and ought—the way things are with the way they ought to be.

One can observe, incidentally, the same use of the notion of a divinely given archetype by Jung to legitimate the idea of divine omnipotence itself. Jung says that proof of God is superfluous because "the idea of an all-powerful divine Being is present everywhere, unconsciously if not consciously, because it is an archetype" (*CW* 7:110).

If someone were to reply, "I don't think of God as all-powerful," Jung has already prepared the refutation: "Unconsciously you do." This idea of God is thus protected from challenge from some other idea of God, which Jung has already dismissed as a stupid and inappropriate product of the "enlightened" intellect (*CW* 7:110).

A third problem with Jung's idea of God is that it implies that human consciousness has no freedom over against its unconscious roots. For example, the traditional Christian doctrine, which says that God is only good so that (according to Jung) the dark side of God is attributed to human beings, is said to have "the absurd result that the creature is placed in opposition to its creator and a positively cosmic or daemonic grandeur in evil is imputed to man" (*CW* 11:739). It is absurd, in other words, to attribute this kind of autonomy to the creature. Jung refers to us elsewhere as, in relation to the creator, the "powerless creature" (*CW* 11:661), and says that "each of us is equipped with a psychic deposition that limits our freedom in high degree and makes it practically illusory" (*CW* 11:143). These descriptions imply that consciousness is almost if not totally determined by unconscious processes.

And yet that doctrine would run counter to Jung's explicit beliefs that lie at the heart of his entire project. He says that the archetypes and consciousness each have some autonomy over against each other (*CW* 11:758), and that one should not overestimate the importance of the unconscious in determining the ego (*CW* 9/II:11). And he even speaks of the conscious mind as "the most powerful weapon ever devised by nature" (*CW* 11:787). A central feature of Jung's therapeutic strategy involved personifying unconscious contents to strip them of their power, and in this regard he says: "in the final analysis the decisive factor is always consciousness" (*MDR* 187). The goal is to avoid being "the unresisting shuttlecock of unconscious forces" (*CW* 7:395). Jung thereby manifested the same problem that bedeviled the traditional theologians: he spoke of God as all-powerful, as determining all things, yet he could not help speaking of human beings as having power distinct from God's, so that they are not mere puppets thereof. He even suggested, in saying that our purpose is to create more and more consciousness, that "just as the unconscious affects us, the increase in our consciousness affects the unconscious" (*MDR* 326). This statement implies that heterodox belief (affirmed by process theologians) that "the encounter with the creature changes the creator" (*CW* 11:686).

These problems in Jung's idea of God all follow from his presupposition, which he inherited from his Calvinistic surrounding, that all-determining omnipotence belongs to the very meaning of "God." Given this presupposition, he rightly concluded that the traditional attempt to shield God from direct responsibility for evil was futile. He said: "The old question posed by the Gnostic, 'Whence comes evil?' has been given no answer by the Christian world" (*MDR* 332). That may have been true of the books that were contained in his father's "relatively modest library" in which he looked for an answer (*MDR* 56). It was quite likely even true of all the sources that were readily available in Switzerland at the time. But it is not necessarily true of all theological thought of every time and place—unless no thought is to be considered properly "theological" unless it holds to the absolute omnipotence of God. Whiteheadian process theology is only one of many forms of theological thought that have rejected the association of God with total power.

The crucial move made by process theology is the distinction between God and "creativity," which is understood to be that ultimate reality embodied in every actuality. God, as an actuality, embodies creativity, to be sure, but God is not, and could not be, the only embodiment of creativity. A plurality of finite embodiments must also exist, so the creative power of the universe is necessarily shared between God and the creatures. Each creature has at least some freedom, therefore, to act contrary to the will of God, which means that God cannot unilaterally prevent evil from arising in the universe. The evil in the universe does not, accordingly, contradict the divine goodness. Because at least some iota of freedom extends all the way down, this reconciliation includes all forms of natural evil as well as humanly caused evil.

This assignment of freedom vis-à-vis God to all creatures corresponds, incidentally, to Jung's thoughts in some moments. He said, for example: "An object that has no will of its own, capable, if need be, of opposing its creator, . . . has no independent existence" (*CW* 11:290). Had Jung followed out this line of thought, he might have developed a Swiss form of process theology. He would not follow it out, however. He quickly pulled back, saying: "We should be careful, though, not to pare down God's omnipotence to the level of our human opinions," because that might lead us to say that evil is not in God. But even then, having protected his revealed secret against presumptuous human opinion, Jung added that we need not impute all evil to God: "thanks to his moral autonomy, man can put down a sizable portion to his own account" (*CW* 11:291). Process theology would support this side of Jung's thinking.

This distinction between divine and worldly (including human) creativity does not mean a *separation* between God and the world, as if God were an independent being above and separate from the world, with the world external to God. Whitehead opposed this picture as strongly as Jung did, without, however, strictly identifying God and the world or any part of it. The position of process theology, which can be called pan-en-theism, is an alternative in between traditional supernaturalism, on the one hand, and a Schopenhauerian pantheism, on the other. Metaphysically, God is the soul of the universe, with a universe existing as necessarily as God does, and existing within God. (Our particular universe, which evidently began 15 to 20 billion years ago, is not necessary, only some universe or other, meaning a multiplicity of finite actualities, perhaps in a quite chaotic state.) The universe is the supreme case of a "compound individual." Experientially, God is not an external being who "encounters" us from without, or who cannot be experienced at all but only believed in. Rather, God is experienced, usually unconsciously, or on the borderlands between conscious and unconscious awareness, primarily as the energizing source of forms, as a "deistic impulse of energy" (*MT* 104). These energized forms, as possibilities for actualization, can be experienced in different ways— for example, as prevenient grace, empowering us to move beyond the past, and as judgment upon the past. In Whitehead's words: "There are experiences of ideals—of ideals entertained, of ideals aimed at, of ideals achieved, of ideals defaced. This is the experience of the deity of the universe" (*MT* 103). Elsewhere Whitehead remarks that, although the divinely derived ideal form is the best for that situation, the best in some situations is bad: "then the ruthlessness of God can be personified as *Até,* the goddess of mischief. The chaff is burnt" (*PR* 244). Process theology, accordingly, presents an account of God that resonates with much of Jung's own intuition about the divine.

Another important principle of process theology is that the more value a type of experience can realize, the more creative power it must embody. Living things have more power than nonliving; conscious things more than unconscious; the self-conscious creatures still more. This doctrine thus makes God's existence and goodness compatible not only with some evil, but with the vast amount of evil that results from distinctively human behavior. This correlation between value and power is taken to be not an arbitrary principle, decided perhaps by the will of God, but a metaphysical principle, inherent in the very nature of things.[35]

This doctrine that the world's creativity is inherent to the world, not under God's control, and that the higher creatures, especially human beings, have more creative energy than lower ones, provides the basis for giving some meaning to the image of the devil in the popular imagination. In the popular mind, the devil is not *merely* a creature of God, in the sense of being a mere agent of God's "left hand." The devil *is* a creature, not a second deity, to be sure, but also something more than a creature, with some real autonomy over against God. The devil is thereby a real, not merely a mock, adversary. Jung himself recognized that the idea that the devil is autonomous "is much more in keeping with his role as the adversary of Christ and with the psychological reality of evil" (*CW* 11:248). Process theology can do justice to this mythological idea in terms of the distinctively human level of creative energy. Only creativity at this high level is capable of really horrendous evil—evil that involves enormous destructive power used in ways that run in complete opposition to the will of the good creator and that, now, threaten the very survival of life itself. This is demonic evil. This human level of creativity, which can become demonic, is a creature: without God's persuasion, which urged on the evolutionary process, human beings and thereby this extreme degree of creaturely power would not have emerged. But now that human beings, with their high degree of power, do exist, their power cannot be unilaterally prevented from becoming demonic. The demonic is thus a creature and yet, because of its autonomy, more than a creature.

This distinction between God and creativity also provides a foundation for the interpretation of archetypes in terms of innumerable past repetitions, defended in section VIII. This interpretation, which roots them in the causal influence exerted by past creatures, instead of directly in the activity of the divine power, removes from archetypes any automatic divine sanction. On this interpretation, archetypes *may* somewhat directly reflect a divinely inspired idea. But they also might not, being instead created from other sources, as feminists suspect of Jung's archetypes of the feminine and the anima, and as process theologians suspect of Jung's archetype of God as omnipotent. That is, certain types of experiences would have become prevalent, even typical, in societies of the past because of contingent, socially conditioned factors. Through the countless repetitions of these experiences, they would have built up great power to impress themselves upon the unconscious experience of contemporary people. But they would not thereby be "eternal," and would not directly reflect the will of our Creator.

The brain, as Jung suggested, would have its role to play in this process. In the first place, as Jung sometimes suggested, archetypal images would be present not only in the human unconscious, but in the unconscious experience of lower creatures, perhaps all the way down. The cells constituting the brain might, therefore, be said to embody archetypes that would be impressed upon the psyche continuously. In the second place, the psyche affects the brain as well as vice versa. All those archetypes in the human unconscious that did not originate from its brain would, therefore, perhaps be somehow impressed upon the brain by the psyche.

This interpretation does not dissociate archetypes from God altogether. Archetypes all reflect what Whitehead called "eternal objects," and all these eternal possibilities or forms are, by the ontological principle, primordially rooted in God. But *all* eternal forms, not only those preferred by the Creator at a particular time and place, are primordially present in God, and are therefore in a sense derived from God when they first become manifest in the world. To be derived from God in this sense does not imply divine sanction. Furthermore, forms that were appropriate at one time may no longer be appropriate. Time makes ancient good uncouth. Or, in Whitehead's words, "The pure conservative is fighting against the essence of the universe" (*AI* 274). This is because "we must conceive the Divine Eros as the active entertainment of all ideals, with the urge to their finite realization, each in its due season" (*AI* 277). There is agreement with Schopenhauer and Jung this far: the forms originally are derived from an appetite, or urge, of cosmic scope. But process theology diverges by not making God omnipotent, and by consistently attributing partially autonomous causality to past events, thereby making any archetypes that emerge neither unchanging nor divinely authorized.

The following question might be raised about this reconception of God: Granted that some of the problematic aspects of Jung's own theology are thereby overcome, are not its strengths also lost? One strength, almost universally emphasized, is that Jung's account helps us acknowledge and thereby deal with the evil in ourselves. As Demaris Wehr says of his theory: "The consequent absence of moralistic condemnation as a response to the evil in ourselves is . . . valuable, and indeed, is the first step toward self-acceptance and transformation."[36] Although Jung himself thought that this strength depended upon regarding God as being, like us, divided between good and evil impulses, I do not. Nor evidently does Wehr, who refers to "his *method* of differentiating oneself from unconscious contents," which "gives us a greater awareness of the unconscious pulls operating on us."[37] The crucial issue, in other words, is whether one is taught to regard the evil impulses as somehow originating deep within oneself. This belief produces a sense of shame and guilt and a reluctance to acknowledge these impulses to oneself, let alone to others, because to do so would be to acknowledge that one was evil at the very core of one's being. If one is taught, by contrast, that these impulses, at least many of them, are inherited, willy-nilly, through one's unconscious prehensions of the past, one can examine these impulses and images somewhat objectively, comparing notes with other people and discussing how to transcend their power. Through this latter interpretation, one is responsible not for originally having these experiences, but only for how one deals with them. This interpretation is not weakened by not having a partly demonic God. It is in fact strengthened by having a concept of God as entirely on one's side against the oppressive dimensions of the power of the past.

This idea of God embodies the aspect of Jung's concept of God that seemed most valuable: the idea that God does not simply sanction the orthodox theology and morality of our day, but often leads people to challenge it. Whitehead was as contemptuous of narrow-minded moralism as Jung was. But, although the good toward which Whitehead's God leads people is a larger, riskier notion of "the good" than the conservative or even the conventional liberal mind can accept, it is nevertheless entirely good, not some demonic combination of good and evil. We need not think of a Dr. Strangegod,[38] a creative power that is divided against itself and is therefore, with its left hand, urging us into rape, drug addiction, war, and mass murder.[39] We can have depth without those things.

The other major value Jung derived from his view of the divine was a sense of the meaning of human life. Much of his intuition can be retained in process theology. Although God is not thought to be unconscious, so that our consciousness is not the first consciousness in the universe and is therefore not, as it were, the Creator becoming conscious of the world it has brought about, our consciousness can, nevertheless, be regarded as of extreme importance in the nature of things. And this importance goes far beyond the point on which Jung focused, namely, that our conscious perception of the rest of the creation brings into existence the phenomenal world. The depth and quality of our experience itself—including especially its efforts to discover the truth of things, to realize beauty, and to bring more goodness into being—can be regarded as divine service. In Whitehead's words: truth, beauty, and goodness "partake in the highest ideal of satisfaction possible for actual realization" and can therefore be thought to provide "the final contentment for the Eros of the Universe" (*AI* 11).

IX. Science, Philosophy, and Method

The feature of Jung's thought that might seem most to preclude a fruitful dialogue between archetypal psychology and any philosophical approach is Jung's claim that, as a "scientist" and therefore an "empiricist," he was doing something entirely different from philosophers, especially metaphysicians, whom he described contemptuously as "people who for one reason or another think they know about unknowable things in the Beyond" (*CW* 18:1503). And yet no feature of Jung's thought has been subject to more criticism, even from his admirers, than his methodological discussions. For example, Edward Whitmont says:

> In asking to be considered as a pure empiricist, Jung takes the very same position he refused to Freud. . . . Jung could as little be an empiricist as Freud, or as anyone else. Like everyone else, Jung's formulations are bound to be influenced by his personal psychology and philosophy, specifically, in his case, by his introverted emphasis and his suspicions about theology, colored by the problematic relationship to his father, a theologian. To this we may add the need to be accepted by fellow scientists of the late nineteenth-century tradition with its Cartesian and positivist bias.[40]

James Heisig's book-length study of Jung's psychology of religion focuses primarily upon this methodological question, and comes to negative conclusions. Although Jung "thought he had presented an adequate methodology that would protect his theories from the charge of philosophical naïveté and recommend them as scientifically sound," Heisig says, there exists "a fundamental incommensurability between Jung's psychological method and the kind of philosophical claims he made for it."[41] Heisig points out that Jung criticizes metaphysics by defining it as philosophical speculation about the unknowable, thereby giving a Kantian definition that no one claiming to be a metaphysician would accept. (Whitehead, for example, in defining the scope of speculative philosophy, says that it should seek to include only "that which communicates with immediate matter of fact," because what does not so communicate is unknowable and therefore unknown [PR 4].) Jung's acceptance, at least verbally, of Kant's epistemology contributes to much of the confusion in Jung's methodological statements, and to much of the tension between these statements and his actual practice. As Heisig says about Jung's failure to deal adequately with a wide range of problems, "Jung merely presumed that a nod in the direction of the Kantian critique would suffice."[42] The most common problem associated with Jung's appeal to Kant is his rejection of going beyond the phenomena of consciousness to things in themselves, followed by the repeated practice of doing just that.[43]

The methodological confusions in Jung's writings seem to stem primarily from the following factors, some of which are in tension with others. First, a deep passion to discover psychological facts. Second, an acceptance, at least at times, of Kant's idea that our "theoretical" or "scientific" ideas are limited to knowledge about sensory data, so that we can have knowledge only about the psyche and its products, not about other things as they are in themselves (except that, for some mysterious reason, we can be confident that something beyond our perceptions does really exist). With this distinction comes a tendency to divide topics into those in which rather complete knowledge is possible and those where no knowledge is possible (as distinct from thinking in terms of a continuum of more and less probability). Third, a desire to be accepted as a "scientist" by positivistic scientists, which led him to describe himself as one who sticks to "establishing facts which can be observed and proved" (CW 11:454). Fourth, a recognition that he was doing more than simply giving "facts," but was also providing a theoretical framework for interpreting and finding facts. Accordingly, in the pages following the quotation just given, Jung says that empirical work culminates in "the discovery and verification of provable facts and their hypothetical interpretation," and he explains that every science needs hypotheses and models (CW 11:455, 460). Finally, a desire for an overarching worldview that not only supports his scientific hypotheses but also provides a more realistic answer than traditional theology did to the question of the origin and meaning of human life. He justifies this type of total hypothesis in the same way as he does the more limited ones. After saying, for example, that we cannot know the answer to the question about life after death, so that "we must necessarily abandon it as an intellectual problem," he says that, if an idea is offered to him, perhaps from dreams or myths, he should take note of it. "I even ought to build up a conception on the basis of such hints, even though it will forever remain a hypothesis which I know cannot be proved" (*MDR* 301–2). In other words, he ought to engage in the task of speculative metaphysics—so long as this enterprise is not defined tendentiously either as the attempt to gain absolute certainty or as the attempt to know the absolutely unknowable.

Whitehead, who was a theoretical physicist before becoming a speculative philosopher, provides a framework in terms of which Jung's actual procedure can be made consistent with defensible methodological prescriptions. I will mention three points. First, it is recognized by Whitehead that all fruitful thought about the world, whether called "science" or "philosophy," has both empirical and rational dimensions, and that any attempt to provide answers to big questions must engage in speculation. Whitehead compares such thought to the flight of an airplane, which takes off from a particular airport—some set of facts— then flies around in the sky of imaginative generalization, then lands at another airport to check the generalizations with another set of facts before taking off again (*PR* 5). Second, although he recognized with Kant that sensory perceptions are physiologically and psychologically (and even socially) constructed, and that sensory percepts by themselves do not tell us about causality or even an actual world beyond ourselves, Whitehead adds that sensory perception is rooted in a more primitive form of perception, called "perception in the mode of causal efficacy," in which other things are given and in which causality is thereby felt. The world beyond ourselves is, in other words, not entirely unknown and unknowable, because it "communicates with immediate matter of fact" (which is why even Kant had confidence that a real world existed behind his sensory perceptions). Third, instead of thinking in terms of a dichotomy between infallible knowledge, on the one hand, and baseless speculations, on the other, Whitehead regards all conscious knowledge, and certainly all attempts to *formulate* such knowledge verbally, as fallible, and then thinks in terms of a continuum of probability. At one end are those items of belief of which we can be most confident; at the other end are speculations that are not entirely baseless, insofar as they have *some* evidential basis and cohere with the other beliefs, but which should be held with the utmost tentativeness. And there is no line on this spectrum that separates "scientific" from "philosophical" beliefs. Some scientific beliefs, such as those about the origin of our universe or its ultimate constituents, may be highly speculative, whereas some philosophical beliefs, such as the belief that we and other people are partly free, may be appropriately held with strong conviction.

There would be many other points to discuss, but these are perhaps enough to indicate that, had Jung had this type of scientific philosophy available to him, he might have developed a rationale for his work that would have led to less alienation of archetypal psychology from the academic community. Because of the positivism of the time, to be sure, Whiteheadian thought was also ignored by most of the academy (even though it always maintained more of a toehold than Jungian thought did). But now that the philosophy of science, in these post-Kuhnian times, has caught up with the position Whitehead had enunciated around 1930, that situation is changing. An archetypal psychology developed in the framework of Whiteheadian philosophy might finally become accepted within academic departments of psychology.

X. Hillman's Archetypal Psychology

Whereas I have thus far used "archetypal psychology" in the broad sense to refer to Jungian (including neo- or post-Jungian) psychology in general, especially that of Jung himself, I use it henceforth to refer to archetypal psychology in the more particular sense of that neo- or post-Jungian movement associated with James Hillman, who began using the term in 1970.

Hillman does not seek to play a role similar to that which had been played by Jung in earlier generations, that of being the single font of insight for the movement. Indeed, he stresses the many strands that have been woven together, seeing this pluralistic foundation as appropriate for the more "polytheistic . . . post-modern" nature of this movement (*AP* 54). Hillman is, nevertheless, clearly the dominant figure and the chief theoretician of this movement, and my discussion will focus almost entirely on his thought.

The distinctive emphases of Hillman's brand of archetypal psychology change the issues for dialogue with process theology. The negative side of Hillman's program has been, as he says in his paper herein (215), "to annul [Jung's] metaphysics so as not to lose his psychology." The result has been to remove those aspects of Jung's metaphysical theology that happen to be problematic from the point of view of process theology. The equation of the collective unconscious, or at least the archetypal image of the Self, with the God-archetype, and indeed with (the one, all-powerful) God, is rejected in favor of a "polytheistic psychology" in which all the archetypes are treated with parity,[44] and the Schopenhauerian cosmic creator is not in view. This modification removes, for one thing, the basis for trust in messages from the unconscious as revelations from *the* divine reality itself (*S 1971*: 203). The more pluralistic approach also removes the basis for "the theological obsession with evil" (ibid.), because evil is an acute problem for theodicy only within a framework of a monotheistic context that is virtually monistic. Furthermore, Hillman rejects the idea of a *unus mundus,* at least the idea of a noumenal world in which all times and places are one, which lies behind the notion of synchronicity (*S 1971*: 193). In Hillman's approach, finally, there is no Kantian, noumenal archetype-in-itself behind the archetypal image (*AP* 3, 13). This deletion removes the basis for thinking of archetypes as eternal, unchanging patterns that are divinely sanctioned by the creator of the world. The way is thereby opened for thinking of them as historically and socially conditioned— even if Hillman himself does not do so, but instead thinks of them phenomenally, aesthetically, and valuationally, generally ignoring the question of origin.

Accordingly, all those aspects of Jung's metaphysical theology that I mentioned above as standing in opposition to process theology's ideas, thereby possibly preventing any union between the two movements, are gone. At the same time, at least most of those postmodern features of Jung's thought which are appreciated by process theology are affirmed by Hillman, such as the freedom or spontaneity of the psyche, along with its purposiveness and power; the importance of depth; the emotional nature of ideas and images; and a nondualistic view in which soul is attributed to all things, not just humans. The way would seem to be clear, at least in principle, for a neat division of labor: archetypalists would provide the empirical psychology, while process thinkers would provide the cosmology, theology, and metaphysics. But all may not be so simple.

Hillman has annulled Jung's metaphysical-theological ideas not by rejecting them as false and replacing them with better ideas, but by rejecting metaphysics, cosmology, and theology altogether. This rejection is based on a distinction between "soul" and "spirit." Soul lives in terms of images and fantasies, not in terms of literal beliefs about the world. "The dream is taken as the paradigm of the psyche," and from the dream "one may assume that the psyche is fundamentally concerned with its imaginings and only secondarily concerned with subjective experiences in the dayworld" (*AP* 28). The spirit, by contrast, is concerned with literal truth about objectivity and, accordingly, develops science, cosmology, metaphysics, theology, and ethics (*AP* 25).

This distinction between soul and spirit, and thus between psychology and philosophical theology, could be understood simply as a division of labor, which would create no problem as long as one recognized soul and spirit as equally real and their needs equally important to be met; but sometimes Hillman seems to say that soul and spirit are not only distinct but also separate, even antagonistic. For example, he has said that the literal is the enemy (*RVP* 48, 175), and has seemingly advocated that all objective statements about the world and action in it be "seen through," meaning deliteralized: "all events are regarded from a dream-viewpoint, as if they were images" (*AP* 45). (This feature of Hillman's thought has evoked, from a generally sympathetic critic, the comment: "Archetypal psychology must stop its misguided attempt to deliteralize everything."[45]) Hillman has also suggested that engagement in theology or metaphysics is diversionary, being a way to avoid the one truly important task, that of psychologizing (*RVP* 136). He has said that the soul's desire for self-knowledge can best be satisfied in terms of its own constitution, which means in terms of images, not philosophical concepts—by imagining itself rather than defining itself (*AP* 20–21). He accordingly says that "soul" is a perspective, not a substance or a thing (*RVP* x), and says that his talk about soul is metaphorical, not ontological (*AP* 19). Hillman, like process theologians, wants to respond to the "appeal of the psyche for help against the crushing impersonalization of the universe." Yet he says this help will come not from a metaphysical position (which would include process theology's panexperientialism), but only from a new "state of the soul itself" (*RVP* 48). In harmony with this preference for soul in distinction from spirit is Hillman's rejection of Jung's attempt to have archetypal psychology recognized as a "science" (*AP* 1, 7, 12–13, 24–25). Also suggestive of a lack of interest in, and perhaps of an antipathy toward, an overarching view in which psychology would be seen as compatible with the natural sciences is Hillman's remark that his move to polytheism "implies radical relativism" (*RVP* xv). This could be taken to point toward a deconstructive form of postmodernism, in which the inescapable relativity of all perspectives forestalls any possibility of achieving a harmonizing worldview.

Another feature of Hillman's thought that might seem to forestall a constructive dialogue with process theology is his polytheism itself. Process theology with its pan-en-theism is monotheistic, affirming (in a quite literal sense) a cosmic soul of the universe, in which we live, move, and have our being. Hillman's call to give equal weight to all archetypal configurations, which he sometimes calls "Gods," means rejecting the Hebrew-Christian monotheism of Western culture in favor of a return to Greek polytheism.

None of these problems, however, is as definitive as it might seem at first glance. To begin with the issue of polytheism: in Kathleen Raine's response to Hillman's "Psychology: Monotheistic or Polytheistic," she argued, with reference to William Blake, for the union of "psychological polytheism" and "spiritual monotheism." Jung's own system, she suggested, "is somewhat confused through an insufficient distinction between the psychological and the spiritual levels." But Blake shows, she says, that

> there would not be a necessary opposition between monotheism and polytheism since the two relate to different orders, each eternal. The psyche is forever and in its nature polytheistic, experiencing the energies of the archetypes within itself; the spirit is forever and in its nature monotheistic. . . . Monotheism which excludes polytheism is a false monotheism in fact really a polytheism which has reduced its pantheon to one! . . . Thus I agree . . . in seeing the eternal necessity of a polytheism; but not as an alternative to monotheism—rather as an aspect of the one reality, belonging specifically to the psyche.[46]

Raine was not alone. Indeed, in his "Postscript" to the responses by readers of *Spring* to his essay, Hillman commented: "one aspect does repeat: reconciliation of polytheism and monotheism—and this through philosophical or theological thinking" (*S 1971*: 230). In his original essay, in fact, Hillman had already left this door open, saying: "The task of psychology . . . is not the reconciliation of monotheism and polytheism. Whether the many are each aspects of the one . . . is discussion for theology, not psychology" (*S 1971*: 205). He had even spoken of "a true revival of paganism as *religion*" as a "danger" (ibid., 206). In later writings he has continued to stress the distinction "between polytheism as psychology and as a religion" and the fact that the many "Gods" are not taken literally (*AP* 34–35). He has said that his polytheistic psychology does not necessarily imply a theological polytheism (*RVP* 170).

Whereas this stance would seem to open the way for a reconciliation carried out from the theological side, Hillman is clearly chary of monotheism. And well he should be. Monotheism has generally, with its insistence that God is all-powerful, virtually meant monism, the doctrine that only one being has any power (and, in fact, because to be an actual being is to have power, only one being really exists). Such a view is antagonistic to Hillman's pluralism, according to which a plurality of powers is recognized. Monotheism has also usually been guilty of Hillman's charge that it contradicts the fundamental principle of life, which is differentiation (*RVP* 88), by implying a "single way of being in the world" (*MA* 264).

The monotheism of process theology, however, is quite different. God is not, and could not be, the only being with power. The metaphysical ultimate is not God, but creativity, which is necessarily instantiated in a multiplicity of beings besides God, and this means that power is necessarily dispersed throughout the universe. Still more pluralism is entailed by the idea that the eternal objects, which are the eternal forms or possibilities, are not created by God but are required by God as much as they require God (*PR* 257). God, creativity, and the eternal objects, furthermore, require that there be creatures (*PR* 225). All the metaphysical principles, finally, are equi-primordial with these other realities, and are therefore not matters of divine volition. This monotheism is not monism.

Nor does this nonmonistic monotheism imply a "single way of being in the world," which would involve an allegiance to a limited set of values to the exclusion of the remainder. Whitehead has rejected "the notion of the one type of perfection at which the Universe aims" (*AI* 291), and has said, furthermore:

There is not just one ideal 'order' which all actual entities should attain. . . . In each case there is an ideal peculiar to each particular actual entity. [It should be remembered here that an actual entity is not an enduring individual, but a momentary "occasion of experience."] . . . The notion of one ideal arises from the disastrous over-moralization of thought under the influence of fanaticism, or pedantry. The notion of a dominant ideal peculiar to each actual entity is Platonic. (*PR* 84)

A similar point is made in Whitehead's discussion of "importance," which is an aspect of feeling imposing a perspective on things felt (*MT* 11). In opposition to the tendency to equate importance as such with one of its species, such as morality, logic, religion, or art, he says:

There are perspectives of the universe to which morality is irrelevant, to which logic is irrelevant, to which religion is irrelevant, to which art is irrelevant. By this false limitation the activity expressing the ultimate aim infused into the process of nature has been trivialized into the guardianship of mores, or of rules of thought, or of mystic sentiment, or of aesthetic enjoyment. . . . The generic aim of process is the attainment of importance, in that species and to that extent which in that instance is possible. (*MT* 12)

In line with this attitude, Whitehead says that the evil that results from narrowness in the selection of evidence is at its worst in the consideration of ultimate ideas, and he points to the greatness that is present in contrasting styles of life, such as the "stern self-restraint" of Roman farmers and early Puritans and the "aesthetic culture" of ancient Greece, the Italian Renaissance, and modern Paris (*PR* 337–38). The ontological pluralism of process theology, therefore, supports pluralism in modes of human existence. There is not One Right Way for all human beings.

Another aspect of typical monotheistic thinking that is disliked by Hillman is its eschatology. He rejects "the comforting teleological fallacy which holds that we are carried by an overall process on a rocky road onward to the Great End Station" (*RVP* 147). Whitehead, although like Hillman a believer in teleological processes, makes a very similar statement, saying that Tennyson's phrase "'one far-off divine event / To which the whole creation moves,' presents a fallacious conception of the universe" (*PR* 111). That kind of eschaton can only be conceived by monotheists who are in effect monists. Although Whitehead's statement of the ultimate principle of existence begins "the many become one," it concludes with "and are increased by one." In other words, multiplicity is not eliminated, it is increased. The process of creative unification will never come to an end in a being who is literally "all in all." Plurality is permanent.

If Hillman's polytheism creates no insuperable barrier, neither does his closely related distinction between soul and spirit. For one thing, he himself has spoken of the archetype of the "syzygy" as combining both spirit and soul, and has said: "psychology cannot omit spirit from its purview. . . . The job is to keep spirit and soul distinct (the spirit's demand) and to keep them attached (the demand of soul)" (*A* 63, 183). His negative comments about science and metaphysics can be understood as efforts to provide for the autonomy of the soul-making activity of generating and cultivating images. In fact, in a discussion of spirit appearing "as scientific objectivity, as metaphysics, and as theology," Hillman says:

> where archetypal psychology has attacked these approaches, it is part of a wider strategy to distinguish the methods and rhetoric of soul from those of spirit, so that soul is not forced to forfeit its style to fulfill the obligations required by a spiritual perspective, whether philosophical, scientific, or religious. (*AP* 25)

Hillman's effort to attain autonomy for psychology and its soul-making seems, furthermore, to have been motivated by the particular kinds of science and metaphysics that have been dominant in the modern world. The reason he gives for denying that psychology can be "an objective science" is that objectivity is "a mode that constructs the world so that things appear as sheer things (. . . not with interiority), subject to will, separate from each other, mute, without sense or passion" (*AP* 25). This statement seems to confuse "objectivity" in the epistemological sense, meaning an approach that seeks to overcome subjective (individual) bias sufficiently to describe others as they really are, with "objectivity" in the ontological sense, which means a description of things as mere objects, devoid of all subjectivity, with its sentience, interiority, emotion, and purpose. This confusion is rampant, having been expressed most notoriously by Jacques Monod, who writes as if science's "postulate of objectivity," according to which "the systematic confronting of logic and experience is the sole source of true knowledge," entails that "nature is objective," an idea that forbids any "animistic" worldview in which phenomena would be interpreted "in terms of final causes—that is to say, of 'purpose.'"[47] But these two meanings of "objectivity" are quite distinct, and the former does not necessarily imply the latter. In fact, to be objective about other human beings is to recognize their own (ontological) subjectivity (which may sometimes require overcoming our own [epistemologically] subjective tendencies leading us to say otherwise, as when we want to use others for slaves or kill them in wartime). Process theology believes that the same is true for all the individuals making up nature—that the most "objective" approach leads to the affirmation of experience, or subjectivity, in all individuals, from humans to electrons. Accordingly, although the nature of modern science made it seem necessary for Hillman, as part of his effort to "allow psychology to return from its distractions by natural science" (*AP* 55), to distinguish radically between psychology and "objective science," the emergence of a *postmodern* science, in which interiority is attributed to all things, might lead to a quite different attitude. In such a context, archetypal psychology, which seeks to deal as objectively as possible with the soul's subjective images, would not have to disclaim "scientific objectivity" to carry out its distinctive concerns.

The same point may be true of metaphysics. At least part of the reason for the rejection of metaphysics on Hillman's part has surely been the conviction that most if not all metaphysical systems were hostile to soul. This is suggested by his essay herein, in which he says:

> metaphysics has for the main failed the psyche . . . because metaphysics usually allows soul a place no bigger than a pineal gland, reducing soul to subjectivism and feelings, to an epiphenomenon of material nature, an invisible form of a living body, keeping it only human, or according it permanent value only by positing a home for it in an afterworld. (217)

But what about a metaphysics, such as that of Whitehead, which does none of these things? It could be regarded as a support, not a threat, to archetypal psychology.

It might be thought, however, that Hillman's perspective does not simply reject particular ontologies—even if he is particularly hostile to reductionistic ones—but that his "radical relativism" is a rejection of all worldviews as equally false. Hillman, by this account, would be a fellow-traveler with the deconstructionists, rejecting the very possibility of "true views" about the nature of reality. That this is not the case is suggested by an article by Gilbert Durand published in Hillman's journal *Spring*. Durand says:

> The familiar Freudian-Marxist-Saussurian language blocking the entire system of knowledge with which the industry of our universities now pleases itself—must be repudiated on pain of that 'death of Man' upon which Foucault insists. To counter a sterile and inadequate dream-language truthful procedures have to be used. And truthful procedures oppose the axiological leveling of saying 'nothing is true.' A philosophy claiming to be new because yesterday's philosophy is worn out should have a correspondingly new *organon*.[48]

Hillman himself, furthermore, has explicitly distanced himself from the deconstructionist project. This is the new element introduced by Hillman's essay herein. He recognizes that his previous refusal to engage in metaphysics "was abetting the decline of the civilization into the catastrophe of concretized nihilism," and that his *via negativa*, in spite of its positive intentions, "still retained as method the critical, skeptical analysis such as we find in bare existentialism, linguistic philosophy, operationalism, and deconstruction theory" (216). He says, furthermore, that he wishes "Whitehead were still around to take down structuralism and the deconstruction that follows it" (225).[49]

Hillman's new stance, articulated in his paper herein, also overcomes the lack of concern for the outer world that seemed to be manifest in his earlier statements about morality. He now says: "The internal needs of the soul require that its psychology meet the soul's concerns about the nature of the cosmos in which it finds itself," especially now that "extinction is a predictable possibility" (216). Psychology needs cosmology.

Besides the fact that Hillman's formal statements, in spite of initial appearances to the contrary, do not rule out the development or appropriation of a philosophical support for his psychological project, it is also the case that some of his substantive beliefs suggest the need for such a support. Even while Hillman was seemingly rejecting metaphysics and seeking to deliteralize everything, he was presupposing the literal truth of several metaphysical beliefs. Although he has rejected those theological beliefs of Jung's that stood in tension with the ideas of process theology, Hillman has continued to presuppose, as I pointed out at the beginning of this section, at least most of those beliefs described in section II as postmodern ideas shared by Jung and Whitehead.

Hillman rejects epiphenomenalism, affirming instead that the psyche has power. He has spoken, for example, of "the psyche's autonomous ability to create illness" (*AP* 39). He rejects identism, reductionism, and idealism in favor of interactionism, saying of psychic images and neuro-chemical systems: "We cannot reduce either one to the other. They are interdependent and interact" (*LE* 175). Hillman affirms, furthermore, "Jung's view of the psyche as inherently purposeful" (*AP* 43). Hillman also presupposes, and even explicitly affirms, that the human psyche is partially free, not fully determined by its body or even by the total power of the past.[50] All of these are literal, metaphysical beliefs, involving assertions (whether explicitly stated or only presupposed) about what human experience is like in relation to other things. How does one make or presuppose such affirmations in an intellectually responsible way in the context of an intellectual world in which they are not taken for granted, and are in fact largely rejected? It is not possible simply to continue presupposing a portion of Jung's metaphysical beliefs while announcing a wholesale rejection of Jung's metaphysics in favor of his psychology. What then?

One possibility would be to take a "two perspectives" or "two languages" approach, saying that deterministic mechanism is appropriately presupposed from the perspective of science and philosophy, while teleological freedom is appropriately presupposed from the perspective of psychology and morality. But this type of "compatibilism" is highly dubious and can be made intelligible, if at all, only in terms of its original context—the Kantian idealism that Hillman rejects. It would seem, therefore, that Hillman needs a replacement for Jung's philosophical theology. Whether process theology could supply this replacement was one of the questions behind the encounter upon which this book was based.

XI. Preview

This book retains the dialogical form of the symposium from which it arose. The five original essays—by Gerald Slusser, Stanley Hopper, Catherine Keller, James Heisig, and James Hillman—are followed by responses to which the author replies in turn. The essay by Hillman represents a new turn in his thinking, which was not available to the other four authors when they were writing their essays; it is, accordingly, placed last. At the symposium, however, it was the keynote address, and it retains here the element of provocative frivolity evoked by that context. The other four essays are ordered in terms of length and difficulty, with the shorter and less demanding essays first, and also in terms of the movement from Jung to Hillman reflected in this introduction, with the latter essays giving more attention to Hillman. (These three criteria happened to coincide rather closely.) I will not attempt to summarize each essay's argument in advance, but will mention some of the common themes.

As is expected, all the authors lift up *points of similarity* between Whitehead, on the one hand, and Jung or Hillman or both, on the other. The importance of symbol and myth, and in fact the metaphorical and mythical character of all thought, is stressed by Slusser, Sellery, Hopper, and Heisig (whereas Keller lets a set of gynomorphic myths speak for themselves and thus for women). Closely related is the hypothetical nature of thought, including metaphysics, which is especially stressed by Heisig. It is no surprise, of course, to find all the writers stressing the importance of the unconscious dimensions of experience, with Keller, for example, finding in Hillman's "underground" the solution for the apparent barrier between psyche and cosmos, and finding in Whitehead's "causal efficacy" the key to Jung's "collective unconscious." The move to the unconscious is therefore simultaneously seen as the move beyond the individualism of modern existence. This rootedness of all conscious experience in unconscious perception is also related to another perceived commonality especially stressed by Hopper and Keller, namely, that experience is fundamentally *aesthetic* and that a cosmology, therefore, should be an aesthetic cosmology. (Casey says that Whitehead's view, unlike Hillman's, is not fundamentally aesthetic; but this difference of opinion depends upon whether one takes "aesthetic" to relate to sensory or at least sensory-like images, or whether one takes it, with Hopper[51] and Whitehead, to relate to value-experience.) Most authors see parallels between Jungian archetypes and some feature of Whitehead's thought, with Hopper suggesting eternal objects, otherwise called pure possibilities, whereas Cobb and Keller look to the *actual* world, speaking, as I have, of the cumulative effect of the repetition of particular forms of experience. Slusser, Keller, and Heisig also suggest a parallel between Jungian archetypes and the divinely derived "initial aim" in Whiteheadian thought. This suggestion is part of another similarity, especially stressed by Slusser, Sellery, and Heisig, this being the central importance of that dimension of experience called variously *inspiration, daemonic, nonrational, numinous.* Finally, Slusser and Heisig stress the drive for meaning that is manifest in both movements. Beyond all these particular similarities is a pervasive discontent with modernity. All the authors would agree with Heisig's statement that Jung, Whitehead, and Hillman share "a sense of the disservice done to our present civilization by structures of reflection inherited from the past, of being in a critical period of transition, and of the need to rescue the individual from the individualism in which we have trapped ourselves" (174).

As I said above, however, similarities by themselves do not make for a fruitful dialogue; differences are equally important. As Keller points out, if Whiteheadians were interested solely in affinities, they might better turn to some other empirical psychologies instead. Winquist says that "we must acknowledge that Whitehead and Hillman are doing something very different" (206). And Heisig, to whom Winquist is making this point, had begun with this acknowledgment: "For the most part the questions Whitehead is asking are significantly different from those that Jung and Hillman have asked, and many points of convergence and discrepancy that are critical to one side turn out to be incidental to the other" (171). Winquist stands alone in this volume in thinking that the differences are so great as to make mutual appropriation impossible. (Identifying with the deconstructive form of postmodernism, Winquist seeks to associate Hillman with this trajectory, and there is certainly some basis in Hillman's writings for this association. But Hillman has also strongly dissociated himself, as I mentioned above, from many of the characteristic themes of deconstruction.) The remaining authors see these differences as complementary, or at least as not so fundamental as to prevent mutual support between the two movements.

In any case, many important differences are pointed out. The most obvious, noted by all and made central by Keller, is that Jung, the more introverted thinker, is primarily interested in the *soul's* self-knowledge, whereas Whitehead, the more extraverted thinker, is concerned primarily with the *world's* self-knowledge. Closely related is the interesting point made by Hopper, that images in Jung's anecdotes are vertical, suggesting depth, whereas Whitehead's images, even for speaking of the soul, are horizontal, suggesting spatial relations. Also closely related is a third point, noted by Keller, Moore, and Cobb, that Jung, despite overcoming the isolation of the conscious ego from its unconscious depths and perhaps the remote past, was still individualistic in one sense, giving little attention to the influences upon the individual soul from the immediate past—from other people and nature. Keller believes that this tendency has been present in Hillman as well; both she and Moore note Hillman's recent move to a more social understanding of experience. Cobb suggests the mutual benefit: Whiteheadians learn that the past is also depth, archetypalists that depth is also the past—immediate as well as remote. Closely related thereto is another difference stressed by Keller and Cobb, that a Whiteheadian rendering of archetypes makes them historical, contingent, and capable of transformation, whereas Jung and Hillman, although sometimes speaking of them as rooted in history, often treat them as eternal and necessary. Closely related in turn is the point that the divine in Jung and Hillman is a conservative force, endlessly impressing the same themes upon experience, whereas the Whiteheadian God, as Keller and Heisig point out, is also a force introducing *novelty* into the process.[52] Another important difference, stressed by Slusser, Heisig, Winquist, and Keller, involves the role of rationality: Whitehead values it far more highly, giving relatively little attention to the nonrational, whereas Jung and Hillman move toward the other extreme. Another central difference, lifted up especially by Keller, is that Whitehead's diagnosis of modernity's problem is primarily philosophical, and does not have the urgency of the cultural critiques of Jung and Hillman. Most important, Whitehead pictures the "metaphysical catastrophe" of which Hillman speaks as rooted in a philosophical error, whereas Keller, as a feminist, believes that it has sociological-psychological-cultural causes which can be diagnosed through a starting point provided by Jung and Hillman.

Discussion of similarities and differences, however, finally has no value, beyond mere academic interest, except as part of a creative synthesis aimed at dealing with the important needs of our own time. Although this concern is only implicit in Hopper, it is explicit in the other authors. For Slusser, who sees worldviews as myths providing meaning and orientation, the most pressing need of our time is to replace the reductionistic myth of modernity, which has led us to spiritual exhaustion, with a contemporary myth that opens us up to the reality of divine presence and inspiration and to our destiny as co-creators with the divine. Heisig's view, although more elaborated, is similar in essentials. Seeing the classic Western spirituality as incommensurate with the fullness of human nature and with the realities of our time, especially our scientific-technological developments and the intermingling of the great religious traditions, he sees the deep story behind the stories of our time to be the quest for a new spirituality. He values Whitehead, Jung, and Hillman primarily for the contribution they make to this quest. Keller, a feminist who has been deeply shaped by both Whitehead and Jung, sees violence toward women (manifested most extremely in rape) and violence toward the earth (manifested most extremely in the ecological and nuclear crises) to be rooted in the modern "psychocosmetic self." This self is disconnected from its depths and thereby the beauty of the world which could provide soul food, and therefore in desperation resorts to violence to reconnect. For her, Whitehead, Jung, and Hillman are valuable primarily for their contributions toward a "psychocosmic selfhold," in which the "split into shallow surface and deadly darkness" (143) is overcome.

This urgently felt need to go beyond the deadly and deadening views of the past brings us to Hillman's own essay, in which he announces the need, especially in the light of the planetary crisis, for "something further" beyond the antimetaphysical psychologizing he had offered thus far. Here he carries forward, in dialogue with Whitehead, the new direction he had begun in "Anima Mundi: The Return of the Soul to the World." He is not, as the reader will see, by any means ready to go all the way with Whitehead. But he does find important affinities between Whitehead's concerns and what he now wants to say—far more than his former antimetaphysical rhetoric would have allowed one to expect. And in his closing response to me, Hillman goes even further by identifying with the Whiteheadian view of perception.

This volume is not presented as a definitive statement on process theology and archetypal psychology. It is, instead, the result of the first planned encounter between them, and many issues are left unresolved. I present this book with the hope that it will stimulate further fruitful dialogue, whether interpersonal or intrapsychic. I share the hope of the other authors that thought and practice based on a creative synthesis stimulated by these two traditions can indeed contribute to the healing of soul and world that is so needed in our time.

2

Jung and Whitehead
on Self and Divine
The Necessity for Symbol and Myth

GERALD H. SLUSSER

It is a great opportunity and challenge to undertake a comparative study of the thought of such stellar thinkers as Jung and Whitehead, especially when the focus of that study is upon their thought about those two greatest mysteries before us—the self and the divine. Clearly, the thought of each of these men is among the most seminal, complex, and sophisticated of any recent writers and will provide a stimulus to our attempts to understand ourselves and the divine for the indefinite future.

My approach will not be in any technical way to ferret out their specific ideas on these topics and then compare them. Rather, I shall try to discover what it is that Jung and Whitehead have done and what they have given us. I focus on the nature of their contribution rather than its content. In so doing, it will be necessary to give passing attention to method and detail, but the main thrust will be to see their work in another frame of reference, that of myth and symbol. The thesis to be explored is that both men have brought forth for us a contemporary myth. That is, their works are replete with symbols that are integrated by some logical connection as a plot holds together the characters of a story.

In the opening paragraph of Aniela Jaffe's book about Jung's thought, *The Myth of Meaning,* she writes, "What is the meaning of life? The question is as old as mankind and every answer is an interpretation of a world thick with enigmas. No answer is the final one, and none of them can answer the question completely."[1] She continues: "Each and every formulation is a myth that man creates in order to answer the unanswerable."[2] Although the majority of Jung's writings deserve to be viewed as phenomenological and empirical, his thinking continually leaps into a more overtly mythic context as he wrestles in his theory and practice with the ultimate issues of life and death.

Let us begin, then, with a brief consideration of the concepts *myth* and *symbol*. Jung's usage and definition of *symbol* are provided in the following statements:

> A view which interprets the symbolic expression as the best possible expression of a relatively *unknown* thing, which for that reason cannot be more clearly or characteristically represented, is *symbolic*. . . . So long as a symbol is a living thing, it is an expression for something that cannot be characterized in any other or better way. . . . Every psychic product, if it is the best possible expression at the moment for a fact as yet unknown or only relatively known, may be regarded as a symbol, provided that we accept the expression as standing for something that is only divined and not yet clearly conscious. Since every scientific theory contains an hypothesis, and is, therefore, an anticipatory description of something still unknown, it is a symbol. Furthermore, every psychological expression is a symbol if we assume that it states or signifies something more or other than itself which eludes our present knowledge. This assumption is absolutely tenable wherever a consciousness exists which is attuned to the deeper meaning of things. (*CW* 6:815–17)

He also observes that a thing may be a symbol for one person and not another. It depends chiefly on the attitude, that is, on whether the thing is regarded as a mere fact or as an expression for something partly or largely unknown. A truly living symbol compels unconscious participation and has a life-giving and life-enhancing effect. If the unconscious factor is a common or widespread one, then the symbol touches a chord of every psyche and is a social symbol of importance.

Symbols of this latter kind, woven into a mythic structure, are the functional motivators of culture. Every culture therefore lives by myth. Or, if the myth remains mostly unconscious, the culture is lived by its myth. This latter is the case in all primitive and most modern cultures. Their myths go unidentified because they are considered to be "truths," "self-evident facts," "scientific facts," "common sense," "universal values," or are quite unconscious.

Symbols are truly symbols to those for whom they are alive. For others they may be greatly weakened or even dead. A symbol dies, thought Jung, when the meaning of its referent has been fully apprehended by consciousness, or when it has been undercut or radically devalued by a rival understanding or superseded by a better formulation. "Whether a thing is a symbol or not depends chiefly upon the attitude of the observing consciousness, for instance on whether it regards a given fact not merely as such but also as an expression for something unknown." In other cases, symbols may function quite unconsciously, affecting the psyche powerfully but without the conscious awareness of why, or perhaps even of what has precipitated the effect. "The living symbol formulates an essential unconscious factor . . ." (*CW* 6:818).

Jung carefully distinguishes *symbol* from *sign* and from *allegory:*

> An expression that stands for a known thing remains a sign and is never a symbol. It is, therefore, quite impossible to create a living symbol, *i.e.,* one that is pregnant with meaning, from known associations. For what is thus produced never contains more than was put into it. Every psychic product, if it is the best possible expression at the moment for a fact as yet unknown or only relatively known, may be regarded as a symbol provided that we accept the expression as standing for something that is only divined and not yet clearly conscious. Since every scientific theory contains an hypothesis, and is therefore an anticipatory description of something still essentially unknown, it is a symbol. Furthermore, every psychological expression is a symbol if we assume that it states or signifies something more and other than itself which eludes our present knowledge. (*CW* 6:817)

Whitehead did not make the same differentiation between *sign* and *symbol*. He used *symbol* in a more general and inclusive way. At the same time, it is apparent that he was aware of and sensitive to those aspects of *symbol* which Jung stated in his more sharply drawn definition. For example, Whitehead saw clearly the power of symbols for the life of society. "When we examine how a society bends its individual members to function in conformity with its needs, we discover that one important operative agency is our vast system of inherited symbolism. . . . [T]he symbol evokes loyalties to vaguely conceived notions, fundamental for our spiritual natures" (*S* 73). Or again, he writes: "The self-organization of society depends on commonly diffused symbols evoking commonly diffused ideas, and at the same time indicating commonly understood actions" (*S* 76). He also saw that the symbol is the means by which that which has hitherto functioned unconsciously becomes conscious and hence subject to modification by the working of consciousness. "The symbolic expression of instinctive forces drags them out into the open, it differentiates them and delineates them. There is then opportunity for reason to effect, with comparative speed, what otherwise must be left to the slow operation of the centuries amid ruin and reconstruction" (*S* 69).

For Jung, the source of a symbol is clearly and simply the unconscious. And this is no unwitting, unguided factor that produces symbols, for psyche is purposeful, goal-directed, and symbols are its messages of guidance; hence his concern for dreams and their interpretation. The source for symbols for Jung was *Geist,* usually translated spirit. M.-L. von Franz writes: "This 'spiritual' aspect of the unconscious possesses the power of spontaneous motion, and independently of outer sensory stimuli it produces images and sudden thought from the inner world of the imagination and even orders them in a meaningful way."[3]

Spirit for Jung thus means the composer of dreams, that which produces and orders symbolic images for its own purposes. Or again, Jung tried to clarify his position about religious experience and the experience of so-called unconscious phenomena to a British critic in these terms:

> When St. Paul had the vision of Christ, that vision was a psychic phenomenon—if it was anything. I don't presume to know what the psyche is; I only know that there is a psychic realm in which and from which such manifestations start. It is the place where the *aqua gratiae* springs forth, but it comes, as I know quite well, from the immeasurable depths of the mountain and I don't pretend to know about the secret ways and places the water flows through before it reaches the surface. (*CW* 18:1587)

Now the concept *myth* must be clarified. Because Whitehead used this term very little, it appears that it was not a critical term for him. Yet, implicitly, the meaning of myth that will be developed here was a functioning notion for him, as is evident in the statements quoted above, and in his reference to ultimate notions as those "generalizations which are inherent in literature, in social organization, in the effort towards understanding physical occurrences" (*MT* 1). Explicitly, Whitehead often used the term *myth* somewhat in its vernacular meaning while yet implying the profound importance of myth for consciousness:

A single fact in isolation is the primary myth required for finite thought, that is to say, for thought unable to embrace totality. This mythological character arises because there is no such fact. Connectedness is of the essence of all things of all types. (*MT* 12)

One may observe that it is precisely the illusion of waking consciousness that it comes into being by taking as *fact* this separation of things, beginning with the separation of the "observer" from the "observed." And surely Whitehead puts his finger on the crux of the matter as he remarks:

The father of European philosophy, in one of his many moods of thought, laid down the axiom that the deeper truths must be adumbrated by myths. Surely, the subsequent history of Western thought has amply justified his fleeting intuition. (*MT* 12)

It is not possible to understand myth in the context of Jung's thought without understanding its intimate connection to archetypes. *Archetypes* are the unconscious dynamisms expressed in the patterns found in myth and fairy tale. Myth is the language of psyche. Related by plot or story and carrying as part of its inherent meaning an emotional feeling tone, the symbols of dream and fantasy manifest the dynamics of that psychic realm of archetypes. Myth "is the primordial language natural to these psychic processes, and no intellectual expression comes anywhere near the richness and expressiveness of mythical imagery" (*CW* 12:28). Myth is the ruling element of the individual and of society, but in these cases it is not the immediate product of psyche as in dream, but has been worked over, elaborated by conscious and group processes.

Another well-known expression of the archetypes is myth and fairytale. But here too we are dealing with forms that have received a specific stamp and have been handed down through long periods of time. The term "archetype" thus applies only indirectly to the "representations collectives," since it designates only those psychic contents which have not yet been submitted to conscious elaboration and are therefore an immediate datum of psychic experience. In this sense, there is a considerable difference between the archetype and the historical formula that has evolved. Especially on the higher levels of esoteric teaching the archetypes appear in a form that reveals quite unmistakably the critical and evaluating influence of conscious elaboration. Their immediate manifestation, as we encounter it in dreams and visions, is much more individual, less understandable, and more naive than in myths, for example. (*CW* 9/I:6)

It is important to grasp the social as well as the individual functioning of myth, and for this purpose some descriptions from other
sources are quite helpful. In a work dealing with "the systems approach
to world order," Ervin Laszlo presents us with a fine description of what
he terms "conceptual synthesis." It is noteworthy, he observes, that
"every age has produced a synthesis of its most trusted items of knowledge"[4] and that "in today's world, most of the traditional functions of
cognitive synthesis have atrophied and are ignored and neglected."[5] His
description follows:

> Conceptual syntheses perform at least five basic functions in the guid-
> ance of human affairs. They are the mystical, the cosmological, the
> sociological, the pedagogical or psychological, and the editorial func-
> tions. The mystical function inspires in man a sense of mystery and
> profound meaning related to the existence of the universe and of
> himself in it. The cosmological function forms images of the universe
> in accord with local knowledge and experience, enabling men to de-
> scribe and identify the structure of the universe and the forces of
> nature. The sociological function validates, supports and enforces the
> local social order, representing it as in accord with the nature of the
> universe, or as the natural or right form of social organization. The
> pedagogical or psychological function guides individuals through the
> stages of life, teaching ways of understanding themselves and others
> and presenting desirable responses to life's challenges and trials. Fi-
> nally the editorial function of conceptual synthesis is to define some
> aspects of reality as important and credible and hence to be attended
> to, and other aspects as unworthy of serious attention.[6]

Joseph Campbell has given us a careful statement of the four functions of myth that has a startling likeness to Laszlo's description of the
functions of conceptual synthesis. The first function of myth he terms
the *metaphysical-mystical:*

> The first function of a living mythology, the properly religious func-
> tion, in the sense of Rudolf Otto's definition in *The Idea of the Holy,*
> is to waken and maintain in the individual an experience of awe,
> humility, and respect, in recognition of that ultimate mystery, tran-
> scending names and forms, "from which," as we read in the Upani-
> shads, "words turn back."[7]

The second he terms the *cosmological:* "The second function of a mythology is to render a cosmology, an image of the universe, and for this

we all turn today, of course, not to archaic religious texts but to science."[8] And as Campbell elaborates, it becomes clear that it is not in
its presentation of facts with certainty that science has served us well
in this function, but in its awesome clarity that no one can claim any
absolute certainty: we stand in and before an awesome universe that is
not only, as Erwin Schrödinger has observed, stranger than we think
it is, but stranger than we can think. The third function Campbell terms
the *social:* "A third function, however, is the enforcement of a moral
order: the shaping of the individual to the requirements of his geograph-
ically and historically conditioned social group."[9] The problem, says
Campbell, is that, unlike the image given by science under the third
function, there is no one authoritative voice in this vacuum; one tends
either to be ruled by private desires and tradition or to give up in despair.
Finally, there is the fourth function, the *psychological:*

> The fourth and most vital, most critical function of a mythology, then,
> is to foster the centering and unfolding of the individual in integrity,
> in accord with *d*) himself (the microcosm), *c*) his culture (the meso-
> cosm), *b*) the universe (the macrocosm), and *a*) that awesome ulti-
> mate mystery which is both beyond and within himself and all things:
>
> > Wherefrom words turn back,
> > Together with the mind, not having attained.[10]

Campbell believes that any kind of naive acceptance of received
mythology is impossible for educated twentieth-century persons. The
individual is now on his or her own. He quotes with favor from Loren
Eiseley:

> there is no way by which Utopias—or the lost Garden itself—can be
> brought out of the future and presented to man. Neither can he go
> forward to such a destiny. Since in the world of time every man lives
> but one life, it is in himself that he must search for the secret of the
> Garden.[11]

Now may be quoted the remainder of Campbell's comment on the fourth
function:

> Creative mythology, in Shakespeare's sense, of the mirror "to show
> virtue her own feature, scorn her own image, and the very age and
> body of the time his form and pressure," springs not, like theology,
> from the dicta of authority, but from the insights, sentiments, thought,
> and vision of an adequate individual, loyal to his own experience of

value. Thus it corrects the authority holding to the shells of forms produced and left behind by lives once lived. Renewing the act of experience itself, it restores to existence the quality of adventure, at once shattering and reintegrating the fixed, already known, in the sacrificial creative fire of the becoming thing that is not thing at all but life, not as it *will be* or as it *should be*, as it *was* or as it *never will be*, but as it *is*, in depth, in process, *here and now*, inside and out.[12]

The fundamental argument of this paper is that both Jung and Whitehead have, particularly with respect to their ideas about the self and the divine, found it necessary to present what are, in effect, contemporary mythologies, although the one thought he was creating an empirically grounded phenomenological psychology and the other a speculative philosophy. Their differences in style may be viewed in several ways. Two in particular will be noted here.

First, Whitehead has functioned in terms of the mode termed *conceptual synthesis* by Laszlo. His work, while speculative and requiring extensive use of imagination and intuition, is cast in a consistently rational style and is intended to appeal to reason.

> Speculative philosophy is the endeavor to frame a coherent, logical, necessary system of general ideas in terms of which every element of our experience can be interpreted. By this notion of 'interpretation' I mean that everything of which we are conscious, as enjoyed, perceived, willed, or thought, shall have the character of a particular instance of the general scheme. (*PR* 3)

Yet, as soon as one reflects upon it, there are any number of symbols that refer to forms of process that are not more than partially available to direct experience and consciousness. Even as central a concept as *actual occasion* must be viewed as symbol. Certainly *God* in both *primordial* and *consequent* natures is supremely symbolic. The greatest intuition of Whitehead, according to Charles Hartshorne, is his ultimate metaphysical principle, *viz.*, "The many become one and are increased by one" (*PR* 21). As the ultimate metaphysical principle this is the cornerstone of his thought, but it is a *mythological insight* more than a scientific or philosophical principle. As he notes in the next paragraph, these ultimate notions are inexplicable in terms of higher universals. The sole appeal is to intuition (*PR* 22). His discussion throughout, but particularly toward the end of *Process and Reality,* makes it clear that he sought for and attempted to enunciate in his thought a system that would meet those functions of mythology outlined by Campbell, and here we find language much less technical, more akin to what one might expect in a creative contemporary mythology. For example, in the concluding section of this work:

> The world is thus faced by the paradox that, at least in its higher actualities, it craves for novelty and yet is haunted by terror at the loss of the past, with its familiarities and its loved ones . . . so the higher intellectual feelings are haunted by the vague insistence of another order, when there is no unrest, no travel, no shipwreck: 'There shall be no more sea.' (PR 340)

Having thus stated the problem of perishing as perhaps the most acute of human problems, he proceeds to the closing section, "God and the World," opening with an introductory paragraph that makes it clear that he feels his is a superior answer to the problem of perishing, superior to that of either traditional Christian or Buddhist theology. And in paragraph two, he refers to the notion of God in Western theology as "the fallacy which has infused tragedy into the histories of Christianity and Mahometanism" (PR 342). He chooses another course that he finds

> in the Galilean origin of Christianity. . . . It does not emphasize the ruling Caesar, or the ruthless moralist, or the unmoved mover. It dwells upon the tender elements in the world, which slowly and in quietness operate by love; and it finds purpose in the present immediacy of a kingdom not of this world. Love neither rules, nor is it unmoved; also it is a little oblivious as to morals. It does not look to the future; for it finds its own reward in the immediate present. (PR 343)

To propose that Jung's psychology offers us a myth is not novel; many have said as much, both positively and pejoratively. The translator of M.-L. von Franz's fine work on Jung, William H. Kennedy, writes in his forenote:

> Not every reader of the German-language edition of Marie-Louise von Franz's C. G. Jung: His Myth in Our Time has understood the meaning of its subtitle. To those familiar with Jung's work, it will seem self-evident. To readers as yet unacquainted with analytical psychology, one might say, by way of explanation, that Jung lived a universal story, or myth; but he lived it individually, concretely, fully, and analytical psychology was born from this life, which was, of course, intimately bound up with the deeper spiritual problems of the age.[13]

Jung did not, however, as did Whitehead, set out "to frame a coherent, logical, necessary system of general ideas." Rather early in his professional life he concluded that such a system is not really possible of attainment because we have no Archimedean point outside the psyche from which to frame such a system. His denial is specific: "I have set up neither a system nor a general theory, but have merely formulated auxiliary concepts to serve me as tools" (*CW* 18:1507). "All comprehension and all that is comprehended is in itself psychic, and to that extent we are hopelessly cooped up in an exclusively psychic world" (*MDR* 352). However, lest there be any confusion, he adds: "I do not mean to imply that *only* the psyche exists. It is merely that, so far as perception and cognition are concerned, we cannot see beyond the psyche" (*MDR* 351). Consequently, Jung felt that a strictly empirical or scientific truth was best regarded as a "hypothesis which might be adequate for the moment but was not to be preserved as an article of faith for all time."[14]

The work to achieve some clarity about life was for Jung a very personal as well as a professional undertaking. About his thirty-fifth year, Jung found himself radically confronted with the realization that everyone lives by myth—one myth or another. Aware that he no longer lived by the Christian myth, he asked himself: "But then what is your myth—the myth in which you do live?" At this point, wrote Jung, "The dialogue with myself became uncomfortable, and I stopped thinking. I had reached a dead end" (*MDR* 171). From this point, however, Jung began to try to discover what myth was living in him by paying attention to the symbols presented in his dreams, spontaneous fantasies, and visions.

He believed myth and fairy tale to be expressions of archetypes, but to be expressions that had been worked over and handed down, usually over a long period of time. The collapse or loss of myth is a very serious matter indeed for an individual and for a society. It results more or less quickly in a profound loss of moral orientation and meaning for life. It is equally disastrous when the reigning myth, as it is with our nineteenth-century myth of scientific materialism, pretends to be *not* myth but sober fact, and its nature is such as to cut one away from the living source of symbol and myth, the realm that Jung termed archetypal. For Jung, "No science will ever replace myth, and a myth cannot be made out of any science." The necessity for symbols and myth is clear. Life cannot properly proceed without them.

> The need for mythic statements is satisfied when we frame a view of
> the world which adequately explains the meaning of psychic whole-
> ness, from the co-operation between conscious and unconscious.
> Meaninglessness inhibits fullness of life and is therefore equivalent to
> illness. Meaning makes a great many things endurable—perhaps
> everything. . . . For it is not that "God" is a myth, but that myth is
> the revelation of a divine life in man. It is not we who invent myth,
> rather it speaks to us as a Word of God. The Word of God comes to
> us, and we have no way of distinguishing whether and to what extent
> it is different from God. There is nothing about this Word that could
> not be considered known and human, except for the manner in which
> it confronts us spontaneously and places obligations upon us. It is not
> affected by the arbitrary operation of our will. We cannot explain an
> inspiration. Our chief feeling about it is that it is not the result of our
> own ratiocinations, but that it came to us from elsewhere. (*MDR* 340)

Perhaps one cannot say that Jung consciously wrote myth, and he certainly overtly denied proposing a "system" of thought, but maybe it is
the case that Jung's *opus* can in fact function as myth for us in the way
mythic function has been described above by Campbell and Laszlo.
Jung certainly believed that his work was done under the power of
inspiration. "All my writings may be considered tasks imposed from
within; their source was a fateful compulsion. What I wrote were things
that assailed me from within. I permitted the spirit that moved me to
speak out" (*MDR* 222).

Thus, out of his own life struggle, begun in his mid-thirties, Jung
realized the presence in his life, expressed in his psyche through its
spontaneous symbolic activity, of some kind of guidance—a luring,
haunting, symbolic presence. To this generalized source, Jung gave the
name the *collective unconscious*; yet he also said: "I might equally well
speak of 'God' or 'daimon' if I wished to express myself in mythic
language" (*MDR* 337). His medical practice and his wide studies of
persons in many cultures drove him to the conclusion that his experience
was a reliable guide to the human situation. The archetypal realm im-
poses itself through imagery and other effects upon consciousness and
does so whether invited or not. One is reminded of the inscription over
the doorway of Jung's house, "Called, or not called, God will be there."

May not this fact of life described by Jung be in some way closely
related to what Whitehead termed the *initial subjective aim*? As Sherburne as stated it,

> Subjective aim concerns the direction to be taken by the concrescing subject in the process that constitutes the very being of that subject . . . the [initial] subjective aim, derived from God, is a lure (to be more or less completely followed) toward that way of becoming which is most in line with God's own aim of creating intensity of harmonious feeling in the world.[15]

Is it possible that, at the human level, the subjective aim is, or is in some way transformed into, an imaginal process? Recent physics, at least in its frontier hypotheses, suggests that everything in the universe may be best considered as organic, dancing patterns of energy. It certainly requires no great stretch of the imagination to go from pattern to image: the path of consciousness may be that of perceiving or realizing patterns as images. But, with Whitehead and Jung, there is something like intentionality to the aims or images, and both connect them directly or indirectly to the divine. Also, with each thinker there is the possibility that this divine suggestion may be ignored in some measure. This initial subjective aim may "suffer simplification and modification in the successive phases of concrescence."[16]

Perhaps there is some comparability between Whitehead's notion of the Primordial Nature of God, which is the locus of the eternal objects—those forms of definiteness capable of specifying the character of actual entities—and Hillman's notion that "we can imagine nothing, or perform nothing that is not already formally given by the archetypal imagination of the Gods"?[17] And in turn compare that phrase "the archetypal imagination of the Gods" with the Whiteheadian idea that "God originates with his *conceptual* valuation of the timeless realm of eternal objects."[18]

The fundamental thesis of this paper is that both Jung and Whitehead, especially in their notions about the self and the divine, have brought forth contemporary myths or symbol systems. If Hillman's assertion that "we can imagine nothing or perform nothing that is not already formally given by the archetypal imagination of the Gods" is correct, then the thesis is correct. And, for that matter, every attempt to imagine or do anything would be in this sense mythological and archetypal. What is the implication of such a realization? Can it be less than a specific and very important discovery, namely, that *in any and every attempt at human knowing we are met with the discovery that reason rests upon imagination/intuition*? That "knowledge" cannot be logical and linear, but only mythological and poetic? That the universe revealed in our imagination is one of meaningful dance more than of mechanistic movement, and that the dance, though it has form, is spontaneous and hence cannot be reduced to formula or be subject to prediction and control?

We have somehow in this twentieth century crossed over a Rubicon in the realm of knowledge. It began with Einstein's discovery that there can be no Archimedean point from which to measure the physical universe. But the human situation has proved to be much more radical than Einstein saw or was able to accept. He went to his grave affirming a rationally understandable, and in principle predictable, universe. The alternative would be a perpetually mysterious universe, not so much irrational as incomprehensible, not so much an unfriendly, mechanistic universe of blind chance as a universe in which human prediction and control are clearly not possible because there is actual indetermination in the process. Jung also had some difficulty in accepting the fact that his own work had led him across this Rubicon. What led Jung, however, was knowledge not of the physical world but of the psyche. He discovered the dependency of consciousness upon the unconscious realm of images. Interestingly enough, the issue of consciousness has become one of primary importance in subatomic physics with the realization that there can be no such thing as an impartial observer. The psyche of the observer is one of the variables of the experiment that *in fact* partially determines the outcome. With this discovery a whole new approach to science is necessary. This new approach is also related to the discussion that is represented in philosophy with Michael Polanyi's assertion of the "tacit dimension" and Thomas Kuhn's discussion of "paradigms" in scientific thought. In all of these respects it seems clear that a new stance in knowledge of the human, knowledge of God, and knowledge of nature is beginning to appear.

It would appear that a useful way to envisage our new situation is to say that all human knowing is mythical knowing. We perceive-create our world in mythical ways, and these mythical ways are not ego-rational creations but gifts from a far more profound realm that manifests itself to human consciousness as the imaginal process. Until now, virtually all humanity has lived in naiveté about the type of process we and the world are, unaware that we perceive-create mythically, imaginally, our world, that we are, so to speak, co-creators with God. (The word *God* here must be used as a most mysterious image; as with Hillman's phrase "the archetypal imagination of the Gods" it is suggestive of the wealth of creativity in the psyche. Or, as Robert Avens comments, "Thus when Jung claims that we do not know an archetype in itself, he means that we do not know an archetype as a strictly singular entity in the Cartesian sense of certainty, but only as a whole cluster of archetypes."[19] *God* may be thought of fruitfully as "the archetype of archetypes." This may make contact with Whitehead's notion of God as primordial.)

What is new is not the *fact* of our mythical co-creation, but the conscious realization thereof. Does that awareness make it possible for one to choose in any real sense the myth in which one lives? It is probably possible to reason about it and gradually to allow it more and more to become conscious and thus a guide to one's will and choice. Yet there would seem to remain a vast realm of spontaneity of archetypal power, which cannot be made subject to will or choice. This realization in turn becomes a criterion for one's mythically dominated thought (paradigm): the myth must speak of the transcendent domain, the divine as we experience it. That is, one's chosen myth should allow and require one to be radically open to what, for Whitehead, was God as "the lure for feeling, the eternal urge of desire" (*PR* 344), which is made manifest in and as the initial phase of each subjective aim. Or in marvelous image, God is not the creator of the world, in the traditional sense, but "the poet of the world, with tender patience leading it by his vision of truth, beauty, and goodness" (*PR* 346).

In Jungian and neo-Jungian thought, this appropriate openness of attitude to the archetypal realm has been discussed in various ways. Hillman has attempted to do this with what has been termed a polytheistic psychology that gives due regard

> to each and every god and demon; it would not suspend the commandment to have no 'other Gods before me,' but would extend that commandment for each mode of consciousness. . . . Each archetypal possibility of the psyche . . . could follow its principle of individuation within its particular divine model.[20]

It was Jung's attempt to give due regard to the archetypal realm, to the lure of God, that led him to build his tower retreat at Bollingen where he said there was "space for the spaceless kingdom of the world's and the psyche's hinterland. . . . Thoughts rise to the surface which reach back into the centuries, and accordingly anticipate a remote future. Here the torment of creation is lessened; creativity and play are close together" (*MDR* 226).

What is the human contribution to the process? How and in what sense are we co-creators? Jung writes that this discovery came for him while meditating alone amidst the rampant natural life of Africa.

There the cosmic meaning of consciousness became overwhelmingly clear to me. "What nature leaves imperfect, the art perfects," say the alchemists. Man, I, in an invisible act of creation put the stamp of perfection on the world by giving it objective existence. This act we usually ascribe to the Creator alone, without considering that in so doing we view life as a machine calculated down to the last detail, which, along with the human psyche, runs on senselessly, obeying foreknown and predetermined rules. In such a cheerless clockwork fantasy there is no drama of man, world, and God; there is no "new day" leading to "new shores," but only the dreariness of calculated processes. My old Pueblo friend came to mind. He thought that the *raison d'etre* of his pueblo had been to help their father, the sun, to cross the sky each day. I had envied him for the fullness of meaning in that belief, and had been looking about without hope for a myth of our own. Now I knew what it was, and knew even more: that man is indispensable for the completion of creation; that in fact, he himself is the second creator of the world, who alone has given to the world its objective existence—without which, unheard, unseen, silently eating, giving birth, dying, heads nodding through hundreds of millions of years, it would have gone on in the profoundest night of non-being down to its unknown end. Human consciousness created objective existence and meaning, and man found his indispensable place in the great process of being. (*MDR* 255–56)

In a parallel way, Whitehead speaks about the essential importance of the world for God:

It is as true to say that God creates the World, as that the World creates God. . . . God and the World stand over against each other, expressing the final metaphysical truth that appetitive vision and physical enjoyment have equal claim to priority in creation. (*PR* 348)

In closing, it might be asked: What is a life like that actively and consciously lives such a myth as has been discussed here through Jung and Whitehead, to realize in full consciousness that one is a co-creator of the world and of God? The mystical tradition speaks of such a life or experience as unity consciousness, or being one with God, world and all. D. T. Suzuki has described it as a state of interpenetration, of which Avens says: "In the process our sense of an isolated ego surrounded by an alien world gradually melts away. What ensues is an effortless and desireless life of stillness in the midst of the most intense comings and goings of all things."[21] John White describes this condition as the state Buddhists have called no-mindedness. This term, he says, refers

> to a complete openness to experience, unblocked by calculations and deliberations, a pure witnessing and observing of the flow of what "is" without interfering with it, commenting on it, or in any way manipulating it. Directly grasping the world like a child, "man regains his primitive condition, but rather than being unconscious of it, as animals are, he is superconscious of it. It is paradoxical: *by recovering his animal nature, man becomes God.*"[22]

3

The Necessity for
Symbol and Myth
A Literary Amplification

J'NAN MORSE SELLERY

As perceptive giants expressing their views on spirit or self, Jung and Whitehead created contemporary mythologies by using symbol and myth, says Gerald Slusser. My response will be an amplification of "myth and symbol" from the complementary viewpoint of poets and writers. I have no criticisms to make. My purpose is to amplify those patterns, images, or ideas that Slusser spotlights (such as "symbol," "myth," and "meaning") by moving from writer or poet to the reasons why, if one talks about the self and the divine in Jung and Whitehead, one must talk about "the necessity for symbol and myth."

Scientists, philosophers, poets, and fiction writers are restricted to the medium of language to express their inner feelings and thoughts. Their tropes develop from the depths of the unconscious and, through language, "return soul to the world," to use James Hillman's phrase. My suggestion is that *what Jung and Whitehead clearly articulated is complemented in poetry and fiction*. Jung and Whitehead were involved in linking the unknown with the known through imaginative inner images. Slusser notes that neither thinker really created only through what he reasoned; rather, each gave more than he thought. History is made by those who extend their grasp beyond their reach. Jung and Whitehead each created a mythology "replete with symbols that are integrated by some logical connection as a plot holds together the characters of a story" (77).[1] Jung coordinates narrative or linear time with numinous or spiritual images, and connects the artist's perceptions with experiences found in dreams: not only are myths "dreamlike structures"; but also

> a great work of art is like a dream; for all its apparent obviousness, it does not explain itself and is never unequivocal. A dream never says: 'You ought,' or: 'This is the truth.' It presents an image in much the same way as nature allows a plant to grow, and we must draw our own conclusions. (*MMSS* 171–72)

It is hard to separate symbols from myth in Jung. The story is the dream, and within that dream reside the clarifying symbols. Jung's first-hand experiences were with images and imagination; he thought and felt in figurative formations, and his expressions became a science of tropes, of metaphor and its variants, of synecdoche. So, from a literary perspective, one of Jung's major values is his de-emphasis on reason in favor of the modes of intuition and imagination. This reliance upon the unconscious as source is the basis of poetic instinct. In fact, Robert Bly says that a poem is "something that penetrates for an instant into the unconscious."[2] Finding and expressing that instant in language, whose essence is translatable to others, is the task of the poet and the writer.

Poets seek to create a bridge from the invisible to the visible and from the specific to the universal. Wallace Stevens, in "Adagia,"[3] writes: "In poetry at least the imagination must not detach itself from reality." Yet in "Final Soliloquy of the Interior Paramour,"[4] Stevens's speaker adds: "The world imagined is the ultimate good." Linkages with the unconscious are required for poetry to have universal application and meaning. The subject and form of art will vary, however, according to the cultural, historical, or psychological perspectives of the individual's experience. It is critical that what Jung and Whitehead discovered in themselves and in the culture was also being expressed by poets and writers. One has only to refer to Thomas Mann, Hermann Hesse, T. S. Eliot, and Wallace Stevens.

The telling of situations requires not only different but often over-lapping forms, some mythic, some symbolic. Significantly, Dante's rose rippling through the centuries contains mythic and symbolic overtones. The symbolic is created when the creative individual finds an image, trope, metaphor, or discourse that, as Jung notes, expresses a "relatively *unknown* thing, which for that reason cannot be more clearly or characteristically represented" (78). Lyric poetry contains archetypal imagery, and as such is symbolic. Kathleen Raine in "The Poetic Symbol" says that there is a plane of "the power of the symbol and symbolic discourse which Blake calls 'the language of divine analogy.' This language of symbolic analogy is only possible upon the assumption that these multiple planes of reality do in fact exist."[5] She and Jung recognize the "life-giving and life-enhancing" symbol which, when it "touches a chord of every psyche," becomes a "social symbol of importance" (78).

So the symbol sustains the core of the myth and, although individual perceptions of myth are important in literature and society, neither the collective nor the personal contains the whole truth. In this context, Joseph Campbell, whose ideas are also employed by literary critics, documents "four functions of a mythology: metaphysical-mystical, cosmological, social protest, and the psychological function." The last function is particularly apt, for it is to "foster the centering and unfolding of the individual in integrity, in accord with d) himself (the microcosm), c) his culture (the mesocosm), b) the universe (the macrocosm), and a) that awesome ultimate mystery which is both beyond and within himself and all things: Wherefrom words turn back, / Together with the mind, not having attained."[6] Slusser adds, "Campbell believes any kind of naive acceptance of received mythology is impossible for educated twentieth-century persons" (83). Poets and writers concur and, although they rely upon myth, they deny a nineteenth-century view of retelling old mythic stories. Thanks to Jung, contemporary writers view a broader universe that includes dreams and the cosmos. Today myths, fairy tales, and science fiction mingle in the warp and woof of narratives as a way of defining a disintegrated old worldview and describing a need for a new perspective (see Edwin Muir, Kathleen Raine, John Barth, and Doris Lessing).[7]

In his theoretical frame, Campbell shows how the poet or the artist works through his or her own image-making experiences to find the center. Consider Eliot's "the still point in the turning world." Or, in *Ash Wednesday*, "Redeem / The unread vision in the higher dream." Or, in contrast, the culture's lack of a center in Yeats's "The Second Coming" and in Stevens's "The Motive for Metaphor," whose first stanza reads:

> You like it under the trees in autumn,
> Because everything is half dead.
> The wind moves like a cripple among the leaves
> And repeats words without meaning.

In spite of the *Zeitgeist,* poets search for expressions that articulate their perceptions of the culture, and that task seems impossible without expressing the unknown found in myth and symbol. What these poets and Jung had in common is what Campbell emphasizes: "Creative mythology . . . springs . . . from the insights, sentiments, thought, and vision of an adequate individual, loyal to his own experience of value . . . as it is, in depth, in process, *here and now,* inside and out."[8] As in life, artists begin synchronically in the present, then mentally imagine the diachronic order by reviewing their mythical, cosmological, and religious heritage, as well as their actual *Weltanschauung.* In *Four Quartets,* Eliot's speaker remarks:

> What we call the beginning is often the end
> and to make an end is to make a beginning.
> The End is where we start from.

What Jung and the poets find is the divine or the spiritual expressed in tropes, images, metaphors, or archetypes (one and the same). When these contain emotional power they are expressed as having mythic or symbolic proportions. Slusser quotes Jung's statement: "For it is not that 'God' is a myth, but that myth is the revelation of the divine life in man. It is not we who invent myth, rather it speaks to us as a Word of God. . . . We cannot explain an inspiration" (87). The symbolic quality expressed in the God archetype is structured in the narrative of the divine life. In "Adagia," Stevens says: "It is the belief and not the god that counts." Jung claimed that the loss of the Christian myth caused him to ask himself what myth he lived. Then he stopped thinking and started paying attention to the symbols in his "dreams, spontaneous fantasies, and visions." What seems particularly important here is not the hero myth that he found, but the *eidolon* with which he identified. To use Harold Bloom's phraseology, Jung could not be the ephebe to Freud, who still lived, and with whom he had already parted. And as there were no particular giants upon which to model himself, Jung, like Plato before him, misprized[9] the poet as archetype.

What Jung says about the poet, therefore, applies to himself: the poet needs to "turn to mythological figures in order to give suitable expression to his experience." In other words, through discourse with the inner images or tropes, the creative person makes these mythic figures concrete and visible. Jung reminds us:

the primordial experience is the source of his creativeness, but it is so dark and amorphous that it requires the related mythological imagery to give it form. In itself it is wordless and imageless, for it is a vision seen 'as in a glass darkly.' It is nothing but a tremendous intuition striving for expression. It is like a whirlwind that seizes everything within reach and assumes visible form as it swirls upward. Since the expression can never match the richness of the vision and can never exhaust its possibilities the poet must have at his disposal a huge store of material if he is to communicate even a fraction of what he has glimpsed, and must make use of difficult and contradictory images in order to express the strange paradoxes of his vision. (*MMSS* 96–97)

Jung continues: "what appears in the vision is the imagery of the collective unconscious. This is the matrix of consciousness and has its own inborn structure." So, Jung began as an architect structuring and mapping the psyche. The images, patterns, and symbols came to him, as to Archimedes and many creative artists, when he left his mind to wander and to use his hands to carry and mold the stones that became his retreat in Bollingen. It is this process that affords Slusser the opportunity to say that both Jung and Whitehead provide a contemporary myth "replete with symbols" (words or "principles of polysemous meaning") that contain "unconscious participation" and have "a life-giving and life-enhancing effect" (78).

In the concluding statement of his essay, Slusser asks: "What is a life like that actively and consciously lives such a myth" so as "to realize in full consciousness that one is a co-creator of the world and of God?" (91). The word "consciousness" is a key. For in an earlier sentence, he adds: "what is new is not the *fact* of our mythical co-creation, but the conscious realization thereof" (90). These ideas derived from Jung could be replicated in slightly different language but with the same "symbolic" meaning from poets. What Jung and Whitehead knew and struggled with is similar to what the poets from Plato through Milton, Blake, and today's great poets confront.

Consciousness is elusive, vacillating, and conciliatory; but then, from the artist's viewpoint, so is the unconscious or the creative image, which cannot be searched for but must be waited upon. Art and poetry, requiring love and patience, remind us of Whitehead's "Galilean origin of Christianity," of which he writes:

> It dwells upon the tender elements in the world, which slowly and in
> quietness operate by love; and it finds purpose in the present immediacy
> of a kingdom not of this world. Love neither rules, nor is it unmoved;
> also it is a little oblivious as to morals. It does not look to the future; for
> it finds its own reward in the immediate present. (*PR* 343)

The issue of creativity resides in waiting for the inspiration that must be articulated through images, symbols, and myths. "Everyone lives," as Jung said, "by myth—one myth or another." And in dialogue with himself, he asked: "what is your myth—the myth in which you do live?" (*MDR* 171). Certainly the poets may not express it in these words, but they too begin in the synchronic on their road to the unknown. Different from critics, they do not need to find a general theory, a point of view that wraps together the processes of others' thinking. They reside in a relationship to the unconscious that causes them to live out or write out parts of the contemporary myth which Jung and Whitehead defined for society.

"Waiting" is a common ingredient in all creative endeavors. And those who must wait refer often to their daimons. Jung said: "I might equally well speak of 'God' or 'daimon' if I wished to express myself in mythic language" (*MDR* 337). Like Plato and other contemporary poets, Jung uses the word "daimon" as a masculine mediating spirit of genius, need, or desire, a transliteration of Greek Divinity: "one's genius or Demon." In "Long ago I thought you young, bright daimon," Kathleen Raine recognizes:

> I see how old you were,
> Older by eternity than I, who, my hair gray,
> Eyes dim with reading books,
> Can never fathom those grave deep memories
> Whose messenger you are,
> Day-Spring to the young, and to the old, ancient of days.[10]

Obviously, this figure is not to be mistaken for the individual; he is an archetypal force from earliest history.

Campbell, in "The Historical Development of Mythology,"[11] refers to the first category of mythology, pertaining to the earliest period of high civilizations, primitive societies, and folk cultures, as that of the "Daemonic." This spirit "or something not ourselves" works invisibly and appears often as a shape or a force. Of Plato, the artist, and the daemonic, Iris Murdoch says:

The artist cannot represent or celebrate the good, but only what is daemonic and fantastic and extreme; whereas truth is quiet and sober and confined. Art is sophistry, at best an ironic *mimesis* whose fake 'truthfulness' is a subtle enemy of virtue. Indirectness and irony prevent the immediate relationship with truth which occurs in live discourse; art is thus the enemy of dialectic. Writing and painting introduce an extra distancing notation and by charm fix it in place. They create a barrier of imagery which arrests the mind, rigidifies the subject-matter, and is defenceless against low clients.[12]

It seems that Jung and Whitehead had to grapple with their inner daimons, and in this sense they were essentially poets (and I use this nominal term to include all art). Though Edwin Muir says poetry is "a natural thing: an exercise of the heart and the imagination," the daimon sometimes appears to work against the poet's desires. Kathleen Raine, in *The Land Unknown* (the second of her three autobiographies), admits how powerful were the demands and influences of these internalized spirits:

The daimons may have known what they were about; but if I was in their power I was not in their confidence. Yet, I obeyed them, after a fashion; collaborated, to some extent; wrote the poems they wrung from me as best I could. It must for them have been like breaking a wild colt, always trying to bolt for freedom; yet in part I was on their side against myself; reluctantly and in tears and anguish I did what they wanted me to do. I did not spare myself, and they did not spare me.[13]

Recognizing the power of the daimon, Jung and Whitehead had to stop willing knowledge and to let intuition or the creative instinct forge its way into their minds. The fact that, despite their empirical or speculative methods, they stumble or "muddle" into the narrative structure of myth, while searching for a way to find the self and describe the divine, tells us more about the limits of language and the efforts of the creative artist than about their visions.

They, like all great poets, are caught by the divine inspiration early described by Plato. In the *Ion*, Socrates suggests:

For the authors of those great poems which we admire, do not attain to excellence through the rules of any art, but they utter their beautiful melodies of verse in a state of inspiration, and, as it were, possessed by a spirit not their own. Thus the composers of lyrical poetry create

those admired songs of theirs in a spirit of divine insanity, like the
Corybantes, who lose all control over their reason in the enthusiasm
of the sacred dance, and, during this supernatural possession, are
excited to the rhythm and harmony which they communicate to
men. . . . For a poet is indeed a thing ethereally light, winged, and
sacred, nor can he compose anything worth calling poetry until he
becomes inspired and, as it were, mad, or whilst any reason remains
in him. For while a man retains any portion of the thing called reason,
he is utterly incompetent to produce poetry. In other respects poets
may be sufficiently ignorant and incapable.[14]

Jung and Whitehead were scientists and philosophers first. When they
lived in that realm they were, as Plato indicates, "utterly incompetent
to produce poetry." Yet, I maintain that what they created was poetic,
that the realms of meaning and art, creativity and science, expression
and reason are inextricably linked and form the basis of the contemporary myth. Like poets, they tried to express human existence as they
perceived it. What they did was face the unknown and sort it out for
us in a graspable way.

Living in the realm of modern society and in the realm of poetry,
Jung and Whitehead sensed the problems of mythic inundations: "Every
culture . . . lives by myth. Or, if the myth remains mostly unconscious,
the culture is lived by its myth" (78). The courage not to be lived by
the myth is found only in genius. Some twentieth-century poets who
find the resource think it belongs to their ego. Picking up on the use of
dream and the unconscious as a métier for the poem, the twentieth-
century surrealist poet often felt that one's inner life should be used as
subject matter and that the unconscious should control one's work. In
that sense, clusters of images derived from an individual's imaginative
perceptions, from fragments of dreams, or from daytime reveries serve
as resources or connections to the unconscious. Driving each of these
is the search for the marvelous, which in turn focuses on a desire to
break away from the ego's control and to find the boundary realms of
fantasy and imagination.

The poet's search is for a vision that transcends the ugliness of the
external world, the city streets and contemporary civilization, and re-
vitalizes the poet. Kathleen Raine accurately criticizes the misuse of the
imagination by the surrealist poet when she says: "there seems to be a
sort of unconfessed hope that the dreaming mind will organize such
material."[15] Moreover, "their so-called symbols are really only an in-
genious code, not truly symbols at all, lacking as they do the essential

mark of the symbol, which is (to use Coleridge's phrase) 'the reflection of the eternal in and through the temporal.'"[16] The poet needs to synthesize and control the powerful images and tropes coming from the unconscious and place them in a meaningful context. The surrealists tapped the *materia* but lacked the meaning, missed the myth, or manufactured the symbols that connected their images to humankind in culture and society. The surrealists then could not develop the understanding Jung articulated in his dialogue with himself; rather, they joined the collective and were lived by its myth.

The poet can fail to understand the power of the unconscious. But, for those who do grasp its power, Northrop Frye says that creation includes re-creation: "the constructing of human culture and civilization."[17] Basically, each creator recreates his or her vision of culture, or renders the culture in his or her own view. The creator does to the culture what Frye says the translator does to a text. "Each reader, translator or recreator, renders his text into a form determined largely by his own cultural context."[18] In this sense, he adds, "the arts form an extension of our own past, but find their meaning for us in our present situation."[19] For example, Eliot may call upon the multifaceted views of history through "Footfalls echo down the memory" (in "Burnt Norton") in order to find a way to transcend the meaninglessness in life, culture, and poetry. But more than that is the fact that, through history, he developed his own modern mythology, *The Waste Land*, which remains paradigmatic of a culture and a civilization.

So, Jung and Whitehead are remarkably similar to great poets, priests, or artists in that they not only paid attention to their myths, symbols, language, and vision, and let them develop to fruition in their viewpoints, but they paid the price of conscious *devotion*, directed *energy*, and intuitive *insight* in order to confront the hollows, depths, and terrors of their visions. The poet's life is also directed from the hollows and terrors of the unknown and becomes less focused upon the release of the vision, the dream, or the expression. In spite of the fact that all new expressions created by human beings modify or deny past traditions, the poet can only live in, as Frye notes in *Creation and Recreation*, an "envelope called culture or civilization."[20]

The inextricability of spirit and matter comes to these men in myth and symbol. Moreover, symbol plus narrative is myth, and, as Jung says, "myth is the revelation of a divine life in man" (*MDR* 340). But that myth, which is a narrative or story form in which human awareness of the world is linguistically and conceptually structured, stresses the fact of "the congruence in modes of consciousness obtaining between teller and hearer or writer and reader." Behind this conceptual pattern is the problem of poet and reader. Some of our gropings toward a new paradigm have to do more with image or trope and symbol than with narrative or myth. What both Jung and Whitehead had to rely upon were the narratives (be they myths or dreams) that others had heard and retold in order to make their vision or story palatable. But their experiences were deeper, wider, greater, broader in vision and scope than the old narrative tales. Theirs was not unlike Harry's problem in Eliot's *The Family Reunion* when, at the end of Scene II, he is ready to follow the Eumenides:

> And now I know
> That my business is not to run away, but to pursue,
> Not to avoid being found, but to seek.
> I would not have chosen this way, had there been any other!
> It is at once the hardest thing, and the only thing possible.
> Now they will lead me. I shall be safe with them.

In conclusion, an earlier question recurs: What is meaning? Harold Bloom in "The Breaking of Form" says:

> the word meaning goes back to a root that signifies 'opinion' or 'intention,' and is closely related to the word moaning. A poem's meaning is a poem's complaint. . . . Poems instruct us in how they break form (or use words/language in different ways, in order) to bring about meaning, so as to utter a complaint, a moaning intended to be all their own.[21]

Jung and Whitehead, as poets, found a new cry, a new Ah-ha, another moaning to show in language how old myths have new essences, a new stance, the *esse* of being. Jung says:

> It makes no difference whether the artist knows that his work is generated, grows and matures within him, or whether he imagines that it is his own invention. In reality it grows out of him as a child its mother. The creative process has a feminine quality, and the creative work arises from unconscious depths—we might truly say from the realms of the Mothers. Whenever the creative force predominates, life is ruled and shaped by the unconscious rather than by the conscious will, and the ego is swept along on an underground current, becoming nothing more than a helpless observer of events. The progress of the work becomes the poet's fate and determines his pathology. It is not Goethe who creates Faust, but Faust that creates Goethe. (*CW* 15:103)

Contemporary mythologies have been created by Jung and White-head. Mythologies are a necessary ingredient in humanity's discovery of the transcendental spirit. Poets have long known, in Slusser's words, that "life cannot properly proceed without" symbols and myth (86), and have formed these discourses through images, tropes, and meta-phors. Though often denied or ignored, the inner powers of the Self are inherent in the twentieth century and have been brought to fruition through the phenomenology of Jung and the speculative philosophy of Whitehead, and have been complemented or amplified by the poetry and art of the century. Through their energies and devotion, as Eliot says:

> We shall not cease from exploration
> And the end of all our exploring
> Will be to arrive where we started
> And know the place for the first time.

4

Inspiration and Creativity
An Extension

GERALD H. SLUSSER

J'nan Sellery's response is, rather than a critical reaction, a carefully crafted literary complement and supplement to my essay. She has so well captured the meaning and spirit of my essay that I am reluctant to undertake any critical response, so the following is rather an appreciation and further extension. Since I wrote my essay, my reading has increasingly concentrated on the spiritual tradition, more recently on the Christian version of it. What is found therein has surprising and profound resonance with the substance of both my own and Sellery's contributions. Saints, like poets and such inspired philosophers and psychologists as Whitehead and Jung, are grasped from beyond the ego and the usual unconscious forces by a power, process, or insight that drives and demands to be expressed. Their response to this experience may require that they forge, through the mystery of the creative imagination, the essence of their vision. As I think Rilke expressed it, the poet or saint is given *one* poem, and all his or her other poems are an attempt to express this one.

However it may be termed—inspiration, revelation, or vision—this being grasped from beyond one's ordinary self lies at the root of all human creativity. People in the Christian spiritual tradition experience the source or identity of this power as God or the godhead. In *Beyond the Post-Modern Mind,* Huston Smith calls this source the sacred unconscious, "an objective component of ourselves—which is paradoxically our deepest subjective component." Through this objective component, continues Smith, we see things, the world, and ourselves as they really are, in their divine light. The Buddha refused to speak about God, but his vision is replete with implications of the Transcendent. The symbols and myths that form in consciousness, are elaborated by culture, and in turn become the guiding and shaping forces of culture arise from these depths of visionary experience. Because this process, almost in its entirety, escapes the logical and mathematical nets of scientism and positivism, it is regarded as nonsensical or meaningless by modern minds. Because the typical citizen of the late modern world has been so acculturated into the mythic view of reductionistic science, there is profound and endemic alienation from the visionary world of the transcendent. Poets and saints (and, one would hope, theologians, philosophers, and psychologists) face the task of creating, in Sellery's words, "a bridge from the invisible to the visible and from the specific to the universal" (94). Alas, our reigning Western mindset is still too overwhelmed by its immediate scientific-reductionistic character to see that we have been led on a road to disaster by this particular Pied Piper. As Alexander Solzhenitsyn put it, the West today is at the point of "spiritual exhaustion." He attributed this exhaustion to a mistake at the very root of the prevailing Western view of the world. Both Jung and Whitehead transcended this "mistake at the root" and both presented new ways of understanding the human situation. As Sellery argues and I have argued elsewhere, our modern, civilized world has lost its center, its connection with the Transcendent. The emptiness will be filled only if this alienation is bridged by symbols and myth that open onto and appropriately amplify the reality of the presence of the divine. It is this task to which Whitehead and Jung and all other profound poets and writers of our time address themselves.

5

Once More
The Cavern beneath the Cave

STANLEY R. HOPPER

Something is taking its course.
>—Samuel Beckett, *End Game*

Something archetypal is going on.
>—James Hillman, *The Dream
>and the Underworld*

Something unknown is doing we don't know what.
>—Arthur Eddington, *The Nature
>of the Physical World*

The business of piling Pelion upon Ossa (along with Olympus/Olympia) ought probably to be reserved to divine powers. This would involve some redundancy, considering the overall subject of this book—"Self and Divine in Whitehead, Jung, and Hillman." Some reassurance, however, may be obtained from the remark of Paul Weiss regarding Whitehead: "I would say he was *always* groping through ideas and *always* changing his mind. I don't think that there was a definite doctrine that he was maintaining. Every time he thought, he thought afresh."[1] With obvious qualifications the comment may be commuted to include Jung and Hillman. All three are adventurers of ideas, and the regions of the self and the divine do not easily submit to conventional modes of academic cartography.

For my own part, in order to circumvent what is inordinate in the topic as proposed, I shall resort to a stratagem used frequently in literary criticism: designating in each thinker his "representative anecdote," so far as possible. Such an anecdote functions as a proximate summation-image for the author's way of seeing or for the author's work as a whole. It also enables one to place or see particular notions, such as process, self, and the divine, as they stand in relation to the author's work, or to that of others. It also accords interestingly with the counsel of William James in his essay on Hegel: "Any author is easy if you can catch the center of his vision."[2]

I. Glimpses of the Unconscious and Archetypal in Whitehead

In the case of Whitehead, such an anecdote can be seen in an example he once gave in a course at Harvard. He portrayed a child tossing pebbles into a pool of water. Little splashes would occur where the pebbles struck the water, and wavelets would radiate outward toward the edges of the pool. The momenta of these wavelets would intersect and move through one another. The cosmos also is such a field of inter-secting events or "actual occasions," only one would have to visualize the child throwing handful after handful of pebbles into the pool, with intersections occurring innumerably throughout the pool. Whitehead uses this same figure in another context, but more critically. Of a thought, he says: "Like a stone thrown into a pond [where] it disturbs the whole surface of our being." But here the situation is more complex:

> For we should conceive the ripples as effective in the creation of the plunge of the stone into the water. The ripples release the thought, and the thought augments and distorts the ripples. In order to under-stand the essence of thought we must study its relation to the ripples amid which it emerges. (*MT* 36)

The manifold of actualizations and the reciprocal relation between thought and its occasions are both adumbrated and exemplified in this statement. So also the problem of the One and the Many leans more firmly into the mystery of Becoming and Perishing, with Heraclitus and the *Timaeus* reciprocally qualifying each other. The "elucidation of meaning involved in the phrase 'all things flow' is one chief task of metaphysics" (*PR* 208). And "the ultimate metaphysical principle is the advance from disjunction to conjunction, creating a novel entity other than the entities given in disjunction" (*PR* 21). One can see, in such a figurative contin-uum, how "the process, or concrescence, of any one actual entity in-volves the other actual entities among its components" (*PR* 7). One can see also, by anticipation, how the primordial nature of God becomes at the intersection of the processions of momenta the locus of God as the principle of concretion, and how thereafter the actualization tails away, as it first appears, into the consequent nature of God. In much the same manner it would appear that the self, too, in the novelty of its brief occasion, is caught up in the mystery of its becoming and perishing.

Because the Platonic vision retains its "abiding appeal" (*PR* 20) in this representation, and because both Jung and Hillman find it equally ubiquitous in their thinking, it is important to consider to what extent such a vision is present as a point of contact between the three. This point would apply also to the status of the Platonic "forms." And because Hillman, in his "vision of ideas" (*RVP* 120), has declined to look at these ideas or forms "within a fantasy of process," and would "refrain from calling them eternal objects in the manner of Whitehead," we shall do well to consider what is radical in Whitehead's "envisagement" of things.

Charles Olson, in a seemingly cryptic and capricious poem (which yields nevertheless to careful reading), tells us about Whitehead. After 1630, he says,

> . . . Descartes was the value
> until Whitehead, who cleared out the gunk
> by getting the universe in (as against man alone . . .

In the lines that follow he specifies the "gunk" as including mechanistic and technological modalities, along with the myth ("lie") of objectivity: history as information, data gathering, reportage, as over against

> 'istorin, which makes anyone's acts a finding out for him or her
> self, in other words restores the traum . . .

The traum, or dream, that is to be restored is

> . . . what we know went on, the dream: the dream being
> self-action with Whitehead's important corollary: that no event
> is not penetrated, in intersection or collision with, an eternal
> event

The poem then concludes with a dangling brandish (a point to which we shall return in due course):

> The poetics of such a situation
> are yet to be found out[3]

There is also the philosophical "gunk." While acknowledging his indebtedness severally to the great names of the tradition, Whitehead is at pains to qualify them radically. The operative term in most instances is *inversion*. "Descartes . . . conceives the thinker as creating the occasional thought. The philosophy of organism inverts the order, and conceives the thought as a constituent operation in the creation of the occasional thinker" (*PR* 151). The philosophy of Spinoza is based upon "the monistic substance, of which the actual occasions are inferior modes. The philosophy of organism inverts this point of view" (*PR* 81). Similarly, "for Kant the process whereby there is experience is a process from subjectivity to apparent objectivity. The philosophy of organism inverts this analysis, and explains the process as proceeding from objectivity to subjectivity . . ." (*PR* 156). In relation to Hume, Whitehead says: "Our bodily experience is primarily an experience of the dependence of presentational immediacy upon causal efficacy. Hume's doctrine inverts this relationship by making causal efficacy, as an experience, dependent upon presentational immediacy" (*PR* 176). Whitehead speaks of "an inversion of the true constitution of experience" in "the various schools of thought derived from Hume and Kant" (*PR* 173). An inversion of the doctrine of *most* previous philosophers is implicit in Whitehead's famous principle that "consciousness presupposes experience, and not experience consciousness" (*PR* 53).

In the case of Aristotle—to return to the subject of eternal forms—the inversion is obvious: "In the place of the Aristotelian notion of the procession of forms, [the philosophy of organism] has substituted the notion of the forms of process" (*MT* 140). And, although Whitehead explicitly says that the "eternal objects" of the objective species (meaning the mathematical notions) are Platonic forms (*PR* 291), he also insists that the notion of the "independent existence" of "the famous 'Ideas'" is "the misconception which has haunted philosophic literature throughout the centuries." He states emphatically:

> There is no such mode of existence; every entity is only to be understood in terms of the way in which it is interwoven with the rest of the Universe. Unfortunately this fundamental philosophic doctrine has not been applied either to the concept of "God," nor . . . to the concept of "Ideas." (*ESP* 83)

Plato, he says, "raises all fundamental questions without answering them" (*ESP* 117). But Plato's failure (and Whitehead enumerates his shortcomings at some length [*ESP* 210]) was a clue to his success:

he gave an unrivaled display of the human mind in action, with its ferment of vague obviousness, of hypothetical formulation, of renewed insight, of discovery of relevant detail, of partial understanding, of final conclusion, with its disclosure of deeper problems yet unsolved. (*ESP* 213)

Nevertheless, in spite of all this, "we must admit that in some sense or other, we inevitably presuppose this realm of forms" (*MT* 68). On the one hand, without them no relational description can be given either of God or of the world (*RM* 150); and on the other, in "the depth of reality" itself "the universe exhibits a creativity . . . and a realm of forms, with infinite possibilities . . ." (*RM* 115).

If now we add to this account Whitehead's persuasion that philosophy is not a science, that "it is akin to poetry" (*MT* 50, 174), that metaphysics is descriptive (*RM* 86), and that "philosophers can never hope finally to formulate these metaphysical first principles" due to the weakness of language in which technical terms "remain metaphors mutely appealing for an imaginative leap" (*PR* 4), it becomes clearer that we are moving into what Susanne Langer once called "philosophy in a new key." Whitehead makes this perception even clearer when he says: "My own belief is that at present the most fruitful, because the most neglected, starting point [for philosophic thought] is that section of value-theory which we term aesthetics" (*ESP* 129). Fortunately Whitehead leaves us in no doubt concerning his intention on this point.[4] In a passage in which he "extends" the argument of Kant, who "saw the necessity for God in the moral order" but not the cosmic, he says:

> The metaphysical doctrine, here expounded, finds the foundations of the world in the aesthetic experience, rather than—as with Kant—in the cognitive and conceptive experience. All order is therefore aesthetic order, and the moral order is merely certain aspects of aesthetic order. The actual world is the outcome of the aesthetic order, and the aesthetic order is derived from the immanence of God. (*RM* 101)

It follows that "God is the measure of the aesthetic consistency of the world" (*RM* 96). "Indeed," he says, "when the topic of aesthetics has been sufficiently explored, it is doubtful whether there will be anything left over for discussion" (*MT* 62).

As Olson noted in his poem, "The poetics of such a situation / are yet to be found out." A step, however, is taken by Whitehead: "[God] is the poet of the world" (*PR* 346). God is "the Eros of the Universe"

(*AI* 253). As such, God "is the intangible fact at the base of finite existence," and is to be conceived as "persuasive towards an ideal coordination" (*ESP* 90). Whitehead thus distinguishes between God's primordial nature (at one end of the process) and God's consequent nature (at the other end) in the process of creative advance toward novelty. In between, God is the "principle of concretion." But while the language of "ends" and a "between" dramatizes the element of process, it is misleading in the sense that God "is not *before* all creation, but *with* all creation" (*PR* 343). *As* primordial, God represents in abstraction "the absolute wealth of potentiality." Thus conceived God is "deficiently actual." God's "feelings are only conceptual" and, as such, are "devoid of consciousness" (*PR* 343). God *as* consequent "is the fulfilment of his experience by his reception of the multiple freedom of actuality into the harmony of his own actualization" (*PR* 349). "It is God as really actual, completing the deficiency of his mere conceptual actuality" (*PR* 349). And *as* the principle of concretion, there is, as the Olson poem says, "no event [that] is not penetrated, in intersection or collision with, an eternal event." In Whitehead's words, "each temporal occasion embodies God, and is embodied in God" (*PR* 348).

The dynamics of "the creative advance into novelty" informs the uniqueness of each concrescence. Both God and the World are subject to this ultimate metaphysical principle—namely, the principle of creativity. So God and humanity live each other's death, die each other's life, as Heraclitus says; save that God has the advantage of a primordial nature—"the absolute wealth of potentiality." Thus God, as poet of the universe, will perpetually compose the disjunctions of the many into larger and larger harmonizations of the one; whereas the mortal poet may compose many selected opposites into a local oneness, which will endure only for the duration of its relevance. Life degenerates, Whitehead warns us, when any process reaches a stasis. God tries to lure us into greater satisfactions, but in freedom through patience and persuasion. "The world lives by its incarnation of God in itself" (*RM* 149).

Concerning the self, by contrast, Whitehead has comparatively little to say. At least so it appears until he notes, in *Process and Reality,* that Hume describes process as occurring within "the soul," and that within the philosophy of organism "soul" and "mind" are replaced by the phrases "the actual entity" and "the actual occasion" (*PR* 140–41). Thus it would appear that a concern for the soul has been integral to the entire essay in cosmology.

But can we say more?—especially in view of Whitehead's observation that the ancient world was concerned with the drama of the Universe, whereas the modern world takes its stand "upon the inward drama of the soul" (*SMW* 128). With regard to the ancient world, he turns to Plato:

> His general concept of the psychic factors in the Universe stressed them as the source of all spontaneity, and ultimately as the ground of all life and motion. . . . The end of human society is to elicit such psychic energies. But spontaneity is of the essence of the soul. (*AI* 51)

He notes Plato's notion of "indwelling souls" (*AI* 122), but will have nothing to do with Plato's notion of "a soul of this world" as an emanation from a more ultimate, unchanging creator: "the World-Soul, as an emanation, has been the parent of puerile metaphysics, which only obscures the relation of reality as permanent with reality as fluent" (*AI* 130). He speaks here and there of Plato's "seven main notions," which include Psyche and Eros, but the terms are not elaborated either psychologically or mythologically. We come nearer, perhaps, to Whitehead's real thought about the self at two points.

There is, first, the persistence with which he carries his insights constantly into his dominant concern, which is that the essence of real actuality is process. Thus his views of the self are descriptive, and arise out of the environment of process. Process is inherent in God's nature, and therefore inherent in the becoming (and perishing) of personal identity. The soul, by a synthesis of the momenta of its environment, adds a new fact: it becomes the bearer of imaginative novelty (*MT* 26, 30; *AI* 78, 275).

There is, second, Whitehead's occasional references to the "depths" of reality. "The relata of Reality must lie below the stale presuppositions of verbal thought" (*AI* 267). God, out of "the depths of his existence . . . adds himself to the actual ground from which every creative act takes its rise" (*RM* 148, 149). This movement into creative act results from the "urges" of the soul's "indwelling Eros" (*AI* 275), which is another way of speaking of God, who is the completed ideal harmony, without whom the Creativity of the universe and the "realm of forms with infinite possibilities" would be impotent to achieve any creative actualizations (*RM* 115).

We now ask whether these glimpses of the unconscious and the archetypal in Whitehead provide a locus in which a rapprochement between process philosophy and archetypal depth psychology may be possible.

II. A Rapprochement between Process Philosophy and Archetypal Psychology?

From the perspective of Whitehead this rapprochement would seem appropriate. There had been, for him, two cosmologies that had chiefly influenced Western thought: Plato's *Timaeus* and Newton's *Scholium* (*PR* 93). The philosophy of organism now becomes a third, a new alternative based upon relativity and quantum physics. The universe, he said, "is laying the foundation of a new type, where our present theories of order will appear as trivial" (*ESP* 118–19). Let us note the direction of this viewpoint in the work of David Bohm, for example.

Beginning with the Heraclitean maxim that everything flows, he announces his starting point as being similar to that of Whitehead.[5] He concurs that the universe exemplifies the mystery of the process of becoming; he believes too that knowledge is a process.[6] Like Whitehead, he "works in the 'art form' of creation of ideas about 'the totality of all that is.'"[7] The relevant dénouement of his project then follows:

> [T]he easily accessible explicit content of consciousness is included
> within a much greater implicit (or implicate) background. This in turn
> evidently has to be contained in a yet greater background . . . at levels
> of which we are not generally conscious but also a yet greater back-
> ground of unknown (and indeed ultimately unknowable) depths of
> inwardness that may be analogous to the "sea" of energy that fills the
> sensibly perceived "empty" space.[8]

These "inward depths" are then specified as the "very ground" of both the explicit and implicit orders, the latter being identified with the unconscious. "Although we have no detailed perception or knowledge of this ground it is still in a certain sense enfolded in our consciousness."[9]

The multidimensional ground of the orders just described suggests Jung's familiar dream of the two skulls. He was in the upper story of a house he did not know. It was "my house." He descended to the story below, then to the cellar, and from thence via a stairway of stone steps "leading down into the depths." He again went down and entered a low cave cut in the rock. There he found two human skulls (*MDR* 158–59). I pass over the dream's "meaning" (as related, for example, to Freud, or to the ages of humanity) to take it simply as a serviceable "representative anecdote" for a brief look at Jung. It is a motif of going down, of exploring the depths of the inward "layers" of the psyche. He says, "the dream became for me a guiding image" (*MDR* 161), and refers to it as "my story."

> My life has been permeated and held together by one idea and one goal: namely, to penetrate into the secret of the personality. Everything can be explained from this central point, and all my works relate to this one theme. (*MDR* 206)

This dream, with its significance, differs markedly from Whitehead's dream. Whitehead says: "I remember once having the dream of hovering, and in my dream taking the most careful notes." He recalled in the dream that he had had this experience before and therefore realized that he was dreaming, so he decided to "observe all the circumstances with great exactness" (*ESP* 136–37). In Jung's dream he "goes down," while Whitehead is "hovering" a little way above whatever he is seeing. Both are observing: Jung is taking note of objects from layers of past civilizations; Whitehead is taking "the most careful notes" and aiming at "great exactness." Jung's narrative is alive with the renewed participation in the psyche's images; Whitehead's account is impersonal and objective, with attention fixed on the space-time continuum of nature as over against that of the dream.

When Whitehead was three years of age, he was taken to Paris. He was playing in a park, his nurse sitting on a seat facing a broad road and a palace from which the road came. A regiment of soldiers marched from the palace, passed the seat, and disappeared down the road. This incident "haunted his memory in later years." He tried to locate the place looking from Green Park toward Buckingham Palace. Some sixteen years later, he was again in Paris. He was standing in the gardens of the Tuileries, when suddenly he found the very place. "The seat was there; the road was there; and the park was there"—the very place where the soldiers had "vanished into the unknown" (*ESP* 15–16). Here again, the image is horizontal, and contains the mystery of perishing and the move into the unknown. The images persist: the stance of "speculative philosophy" and the mysteries of becoming and perishing.

We must, however, bear in mind that speculative thinking for Whitehead becomes "speculative imagination" (in which reason and imagination unite); hence the grandeur of his "leap" out of the philosophical systems into the new cosmic vision, with its creative advance into novelty. Without a developed view of the imagination, however, his thought moves laterally, whereas that of Jung moves into the depth. Both, nevertheless, are trying to move from the dominance of Logos (classical logic) to Mythos (which roots in experience), to use a distinction of Gary Zukav's.[10] Both would concur in the following:

> According to quantum mechanics there is no such thing as objectivity. We cannot eliminate ourselves from the picture. We are part of nature, and when we study nature there is no way around the fact that nature is studying itself. Physics has become a branch of psychology, or perhaps the other way around.[11]

Zukav then quotes from Jung and from the Nobel Prize–winning physicist Wolfgang Pauli, and concludes that "if these men are correct, then physics is the study of the structure of consciousness."[12] The considerable importance of this parallelism resides in the prospect that Whitehead's "eternal objects" (as primordial potentials) are to Whitehead's "process" as Jung's "archetypes" are to his "consciousness." In the "Supplement" to his essay "On the Nature of the Psyche," Jung writes: "Archetypes are typical forms of behaviour which, once they become conscious, naturally present themselves *as ideas and images*" (*CW* 8:435). By way of these effects we discover that they have "an *organizing* influence on the contents of consciousness" (*CW* 8:439). The psychology of unconscious processes, Jung insists, is therefore not "a sort of *philosophy* designed to explain mythologems," as is often supposed; it is, rather, a recognition of a dimension in the unconscious beyond our grasp, which nevertheless affects us in such ways as may lead us to the point of, in Pauli's cautious terms, "postulating the existence of an unconscious that possesses a large measure of objective reality" (*CW* 8:439n).

It is often suggested that Jung is Kantian in this type of *a priori* designation; but Joseph Campbell quite properly observes the qualitative difference between Kant's *a priori* Forms of Sensibility and Categories of Logic and the Jungian "archetypes," which Campbell regards as the *a priori* Forms of Mythic Fantasy. He then cites Jung: the archetypes "are not determined as regards their content, but only as regards their form."[13]

Jung himself designates the *a priori* factor as follows:

within the limits of psychic experience, the collective unconscious takes the place of the Platonic realm of eternal ideas. Instead of these models giving form to created things, the collective unconscious, through its archetypes, provides the *a priori* condition for the assignment of meaning. (*CW* 14:87)

The archetypes may be compared "to the axial system of a crystal" or, as Jung phrases it in another context, "much as a crystalline grid arranges the molecules in a saturated solution" (*CW* 18:1158). For Jung, this points to the psyche as "an autonomous factor," an objective source to which we can set no bounds, or which, as Hillman says, is "endless" (*DU* 126). Just as Whitehead found Heraclitus's maxim that "all things flow" to be central to his thinking, so both Jung and Hillman find his other aphorism a frequent *point d'appui*: "You could not find the ends of the soul though you travelled every way, so deep is its logos" (*DU* 25). "We can never go deep enough," as Hillman says.

For Jung, the conscious mind (the ego) and the unconscious "complement one another to form a totality, which is the *self*" (*CW* 7:274). Although intellectually the self is a psychological concept, "a construct that serves to express an unknowable essence which we cannot grasp as such," it is experienced as a deep center, as "the God within us" (*CW* 7:399). It evidences itself frequently as a complex of opposites. Its symbols have often a numinous quality. It may also represent itself as a God-image, as witness the claim of Clement of Alexandria that he who knows himself knows God (*CW* 9/II:42, 347).

Concerning "God," then, Jung remains circumspectly within the purview of the psyche and its archetypes. In his Tavistock Lectures, God is the "Symbol of symbols." Elsewhere we read that "all statements about God have their origin in the psyche and must therefore be distinguished from God as a metaphysical being" (*CW* 18:1511). Further, in a letter to the Reverend David Cox, he holds that "the whole metaphysical world is understood as a psychic structure projected into the sphere of the unknown" (*CW* 18:1658). Crucial to the realization of the self is the withdrawal of all these external projections, in order that the soul (which in Jung is more proximately the "personality") may become aware of the deep self within.

It would be relevant now to consider Jung's "process of individuation," but, keeping in mind Whitehead's ultimate principle of creativity and his commitment to *aisthesis* as the mode appropriate to speculative thinking, our interest is rather in Jung's notions about the process of creativity. These may be quickly indicated.

Jung notes, first of all, that great art speaks always in primordial images, and that the creative process consists "in the unconscious activation of an archetypal image" (CW 15:130). The artist

> is everywhere hemmed round and prevailed upon by the Unconscious, the mysterious god within him; so that ideas flow to him. . . . [He becomes] a vehicle and moulder of the unconscious psychic life of mankind. That is his office, and it is sometimes so heavy a burden that he is fated to sacrifice happiness and everything that makes life worth living for the ordinary human being. (CW 15:157)

Indeed, the artistic venture often begins with the symbol of the nekyia, which is the descent into the unconscious, the journey to Hades:

> The Nekyia is no aimless and purely destructive fall into the abyss, but a meaningful *katabasis eis antron,* a descent into the cave of initiation and secret knowledge. The journey through the psychic history of mankind [*vide* Jung's dream] has as its object the restoration of the whole man. (CW 15:213)

Then he remarks that the great work of art is like a dream: in spite of its seeming lucidity it gives no explanation of itself and remains ambiguous. At the same time it aims at restoring "the psychic balance, whether of the individual or of the epoch" (CW 15:160).

Whitehead also speaks of balance, much as Robert Bridges did in these lines: "Our stability is but balance, and conduct lies / in masterful administration of the unforeseen . . . ,"[14] complying, that is, with the creative advance into novelty, composing the disjunctions into conjunctions like someone riding a bicycle: if he stops pedaling, all is lost.

Hillman represents a difference, but in two stages: the one, everything written before "*Anima Mundi:* The Return of the Soul to the World"; and two, this essay itself, and the essay in this volume, in which one sees overtures to Whitehead and an open threshold looking toward Zen.

In the first stage, we see his intent made clear. *"I would remove discussion of ideas from the realm of thought to the realm of psyche"* (RVP 121). "Depth psychology . . . leads eventually to the recognition of soul as the inward, downward factor in personality, the factor which gives depth" (MA 52).

> Our opportunity is to translate the language of reason into the arche-
> typal background of the unconscious and its speech, to change concept
> back into metaphor. (*MA* 162)

Again: "Nothing is literal; all is metaphor" in dreams, which are "the
best model of the actual psyche" (*RVP* 175). And yet once again:
*"Through psychologizing I change the idea of any literal action at all . . .
into a metaphorical enactment"* (*RVP* 127). These affirmations may be
sharpened by two additional crucial statements. The first: "There is no
end to depth, and all things become soul" (*DU* 27). And the second:

> Within the metaphorical perspective, within the imaginal field, noth-
> ing is more sure than the soul's own activity. . . . Thus the soul finds
> psyche everywhere, recognizes itself in all things, all things providing
> psychological reflection. And the soul accepts itself in its mythical
> enactments as one more such metaphor. More real than itself, more
> ultimate than its psychic metaphor, there is nothing. (*RVP* 154)

In view of the above, it is not difficult to understand why there is
little talk about "God" in Hillman's writings, but a great deal about
"Gods." "Theology," he notes, "takes Gods literally and we do not"
(*RVP* 169). "In archetypal psychology Gods are *imagined*. . . . They
are formulated ambiguously, as metaphors for modes of experience and
as numinous borderline persons. They are cosmic perspectives in which
the soul participates" (*RVP* 169). This would apply equally to Hillman's
fantasy of the "Underworld" and its concomitant notion of "death." The
importance of this becomes clearer when Hillman's book on the underworld is described as "the main bridge—or tunnel—into my other
writings" (*DU* 5). "The image has been my starting point for the archetypal re-visioning of psychology" (*DU* 5). The key anecdote of this
work is that of the *nekyia*: the journey to Hades, the descent into the
unconscious. I cite again Jung's statement: "The Nekyia is no aimless
and purely destructive fall into the abyss, but a meaningful *katabasis eis
antron,* a descent into the cave of initiation and secret knowledge" (*CW*
15:213).

It is this descent that appears to be everywhere wanting in Whitehead's "fantasy of process," though his surmises concerning the unconscious appear to anticipate a place for it in his notion of creative advance;
and it may well be that Whitehead's notion will supply a corrective to
Hillman's fantasy of the Underworld.

Hillman speaks of "listening to him [Freud] metaphorically and against the background of the *nekyia,* or the archetypal descent" (*DU* 21). Listening in turn to Hillman metaphorically (and against the same background), I do not hear him speaking as metaphorically, or as imaginally, as his thesis requires. He speaks more consistently in *images* than in metaphors; and though he urges that the underworld images are *images as metaphors* (*DU* 54), they nonetheless have a tendency to become signs and function as concepts (though signs carry a message and concepts do not). Images tend to become fixed, thus literalized and unwittingly idolatrous, if "petrified" (to use Whitehead's term) by reason of stasis. The same is true of the myth if it loses its story, or the dream if it loses its anecdote. The "meaning" is in the anecdote, not in the images.

Clearly Hillman does not intend this result. He specifically says that "Underworld images . . . are *images as metaphors*" (*DU* 54). At the same time, it would appear that he senses the problem when he alludes to himself as a *bricoleur,* thus providing us with his own representative anecdote. An earlier reference describes the *bricoleur* as "an odd-job man, like Eros the Carpenter who joins this bit with that" (*RVP* 164). In *The Dream and the Underworld,* the image of the *bricoleur* is assigned to the dream-work: "the dream *bricoleur* is a handyman, who takes the bits of junk left over from the day and potters about with them, tacking residual things together into a collage, . . . [shaping] them into a new sense within a new context" (*DU* 127–28). Lévi-Strauss, from whom the term is taken, suggests that "mythical thought is . . . a kind of intellectual 'bricolage.' . . . [I]t builds up structured sets . . . by using the remains and debris of events."[15] The significant images of myth, which are its materials, are made up of things that "have had a use" and "can be used again" either for the same or for a different purpose. The nature of Hillman's project makes him inevitably just such a *bricoleur*, picking and choosing from the symbolic debris of Western thought and attempting their reassemblage in a new and different context. The difficulty with this image is that it lacks what Whitehead calls "fusion": chunks of thought become eclectic, an aggregate, but lack embodiment in a lively whole.

But the real problem lies elsewhere, and, in my judgment, in two aspects.

First, the term "metaphor," which is the operative term in Hillman's project, has not been thought through deeply enough. It still functions in its Aristotelian mode of carrying recognition across from something known to something unknown by way of semantic identification. This is what Philip Wheelwright has called the *epiphor*.[16] A deeper form is that of *diaphor*, which implies and effects a *movement through*. This is achieved through the juxtaposition of images that, while retaining their own integrity, nevertheless impel new meanings to emerge. The White-headian formula applies: "The ultimate metaphysical principle is the advance from disjunction to conjunction, creating a novel entity other than the entities given in disjunction" (*PR* 21). One illustration must suffice:

> The marble form in the pine wood,
>   The shrine seen and not seen
> From the roots of sequoias[17]

"The role of diaphor is to create presence," notes Wheelwright.[18] The images in the verses are precise; each one remains what it is. The emergence of presence consists not only in making us *notice* the things given, but in letting presence emerge. As a saying of Sojō put it: "Heaven and I are the same root. The ten thousand things and I are of one substance."[19] The Japanese *haiku* has this same diaphoric power.

The second aspect of the problem: the analogue that we are seeking as an aesthetic hermeneutic is not that of mythic thought as propounded by Lévi-Strauss in his metaphor of the *bricoleur*; it is rather that of the art form, which conserves the anecdote, retaining its ambiguities, enigmas, parabolic reticence, and cryptic depths, yet perpetually propels that movement through into what Heidegger calls the "open" (where Being comes to presence). The art form is not hierarchical, though it celebrates the upward and the downward way. It does not permit its forms to become absolutes. Mythic figures and images must therefore remain fluent; otherwise they become impediments and interfere with the psyche's descents.

It was Nietzsche who questioned whether a thinker "*can* have 'ultimate and actual' opinions at all; whether behind every cave in him there is not, and necessarily must be, a still deeper cave: . . . an abyss behind every bottom, beneath every 'foundation.'"[20] The same holds for images as well. We must break through the bottom of the pail, as the Zen people say. The strategy of the *kōan* is precisely to lead us beyond "ideas" and to dispense with "images" too; just as the strategy of the *haiku* is to release us into recognitions beyond the terms of the poem itself. "I speak," wrote Wallace Stevens, "below the tension of the lyre."[21] "There was a myth," he said again, "before the myth began."[22] Eckhart also, as Jung has noted, is said to have remarked, "on returning to his true self," that one "enters an abyss 'deeper than hell itself'" (*CW* 9/II:209). "Go hence; the limits of the soul thou canst not discover, though thou shouldst traverse every way; so profoundly is it rooted (*Bathun*—one might as well say, *abyssed*) in the Logos." It is just from this depth that the Logos "speaks." All is utterance. "Expression," wrote Whitehead, "is the one fundamental sacrament. It is the outward and visible sign of an inward and spiritual grace" (*RM* 121). But it is by way of the inwardness that speech becomes (as Hillman would say) ensouled. It is by way of the abyss, which we discover is the source, that transparency is achieved. This is Hillman's "Transparent Man,"

> who is seen through, foolish, who has nothing left to hide, who has become transparent through self-acceptance; his soul is loved, wholly revealed, wholly existential; he is just what he is, freed from paranoid concealment. (*MA* 92)

It is also Kierkegaard's *self,* grounded transparently upon the Power that posits it.

From this perspective we see that the anecdote of the dream is also a *kōan*. It is beyond "ideas" and, paradoxically, beyond its own images; just as it is beyond good and evil, and beyond God and the gods— though "there are gods here also" (Heraclitus) and "Jove nods to Jove behind each one of us" (Emerson). It is not unlike the luminous parable of Chuang-Tzu, entitled "The Lost Pearl."

> The Yellow Emperor went wandering
> To the north of the Red Water
> To the Kwan Lun mountain. He looked around
> Over the edge of the world. On the way home
> He lost his night-coloured pearl.
> He sent out Science to seek his pearl, and got nothing.
> He sent Analysis to look for his pearl, and got nothing.
> He sent out Logic to seek his pearl, and got nothing.
> Then he asked Nothingness, and Nothingness had it.
>
> The Yellow Emperor said:
> "Strange indeed: Nothingness
> Who was not sent
> Who did no work to find it
> Had the night-coloured pearl!"[23]

In his superb article on Heidegger and Hillman, Robert Avens sees the two men as "two paths that, strictly speaking, have only one thing in common: they lead nowhere."[24] Like Hui Neng, he then notes, it is as if they were both trying "to awaken the mind without fixing it upon anything."

In his essay "*Anima Mundi*: The Return of the Soul to the World," Hillman appears to be shifting his ground. As with Whitehead, we see a turn to cosmology. He hopes that a way "might open again toward a metapsychology that is a cosmology, a poetic vision of the cosmos which fulfills the soul's need for placing itself in the vast scheme of things" (*S 1982*: 82). As with Whitehead (*AI* 252–54), the notion of *aisthesis* is central. "Beauty is an epistemological necessity; *aisthesis* is how we know the world" (*S 1982*: 84). He includes Whitehead in his calendar of relevant thinkers (*S 1982*: 92). Heidegger is not included, nor is Heraclitus (which may be an oversight; or perhaps things no longer flow, but now circle, or because the "game of oppositions" must be given up "altogether"). "I reenter the Platonic cosmos," he affirms (*S 1982*: 79). He would make this reentry through Ficino, who recovers the *Timaeus's* notion of the world-soul, "which means nothing less than the world ensouled" (*S 1982*: 77).

There is doubtless a certain compatibility between Ficino's cosmological "envisagement" and that of Whitehead. The *pars pro toto* is retained; but the principle of the creative advance into novelty is not, nor does the Ficino vision as an "art form" seem to embody it. It is possible that we must "twist out of Plato" (Heidegger's phrase about Nietzsche) if we are to reenter him. Whitehead sets aside the static side of the *Timaeus* in order to retain the side of "life and motion."

One more reference to Whitehead is striking. This has to do with the notion of "importance" (which Hillman has noted before). This is equated with *notitia,* or taking notice of things. It is like the Japanese exclamation "A-a-ah!" when suddenly touched by beauty. The word *aisthesis,* Hillman tells us, refers to the gasp, the "aha," the "uh" of the breath of wonder. It is recognition of the "eachness" of things, or (let us note) like the Eastern notion of *suchness*. Which suggests that the ensoulment of things has not only Whitehead's *importance* but also the Zen notion of awareness.

> What is the Buddha?
> The blossoming branch of a plum tree.

Listening to all of this metaphorically, we hear a different sound in this essay, along with its different "envisagement" of things. Mysticism? Whitehead? Zen? The Poetics of this situation have yet to be written; but something is going on.

> To build the city of Dioce whose terraces are the colour of
>   stars.
> The suave eyes, quiet, not scornful,
>   rain also is of the process.
> What you depart from is not the way
> and olive tree blown white in the wind
> washed in the Kiang and Han
> what whiteness will you add to this whiteness,
>
>   what candor?
> "the great periplum brings in the stars to our shore."[25]

6

Eternal Objects and Archetypes, Past and Depth

A Response to Stanley Hopper

JOHN B. COBB, JR.

This paper is vintage Hopper. It is richly metaphorical throughout, even in its account of metaphor. I wish that I could respond in kind, but I cannot.

There are scattered interpretations of Whitehead with which I have technical difficulties, but to devote my response to these would not be appropriate to a paper of this sort. I will therefore deal with just one such point, a minor one in the paper, and then devote the rest of my time to exploring the fruitfulness of Hopper's suggestions, especially for Whiteheadians.

In section II of his essay, Hopper speaks of the "prospect that Whitehead's 'eternal objects' (as primordial potentials) are to Whitehead's 'process' as Jung's 'archetypes' are to his 'consciousness.'" A parallelism of this sort is tempting and even suggestive, but I believe it will lead to a misunderstanding of Whitehead and distract attention from a suitably Whiteheadian account of archetypes.

Hopper quotes Jung's statement that "archetypes are typical forms of behaviour which, once they become conscious, naturally present themselves *as ideas and images.*" Now it is certainly true that such typical forms are, in Whitehead's terms, eternal objects. But for Whitehead they share this status with atypical forms of behavior and with forms of possible behavior that may never be actualized at all. Hopper's suggestion obscures this very important fact about Whitehead's view of the forms, namely, their complete neutrality with respect to ingression in the world.

Whitehead's account of archetypes would employ the notion of eternal objects, but no more so than his account of anything else. The emphasis in discussing archetypes would be on the causal efficacy of the past. If in the past there are frequently repeated forms of conduct, then certainly they will exercise cumulative force in the present. This is the nature of causal efficacy in general. It explains the recurrence of patterns in the world studied by physics as well as in that studied by psychology. For Whitehead, as for Jung, the forms that characterize unconscious physical prehensions must become ideas and images if and as they enter into consciousness. This is the way ordinary sense-experience operates. Whitehead did not extend his technical treatment of these matters to dreams and myths, but that such extension is immensely fruitful should not surprise a Whiteheadian. One could not predict from the general theory which images will express for consciousness forms of behavior often repeated in the past. Like all empirical facts, this is to be learned from observation.

My reason for concern here is that Whitehead's use of the term *eternal* with respect to pure potentials has had an unfortunate tendency to lead readers to suppose that something honorific is implied. Whatever Plato's position about the ideas may finally have been, Whitehead's lacks this nuance. *Eternal* means merely *not temporal,* that is, unaffected by process. The process necessarily has some character; that is, it embodies some forms rather than others. But these forms or eternal objects, as *eternal* objects, are what they are whether they are embodied or not. We throw no light whatsoever on why the world or human experience has one form rather than another by appeal to eternal objects alone. For that we must always appeal to *decisions,* whether of God or of creatures.

Now that I have done my duty in pointing out what I see as a weakness in Hopper's paper, I want to turn to its strength. Whiteheadians have much to gain by having our attention turned by Hopper to our basic images.

The paper points to a difference of the images employed by Whitehead on the one hand and Jung and Hillman on the other (section II). Hopper shows that the difference is important for understanding them, but that it does not preclude a convergence of the two streams of thought and sensibility. That is convincing to me. Despite many qualifications, Whitehead's imagery does picture the four dimensions of the extensive appealing for an imaginative leap" (PR 4). The result is that "no language can be anything but elliptical, requiring a leap of the imagination to understand its meaning in its relevance to immediate experience" (PR 13). This is where the understanding of Whitehead's philosophy should begin—with metaphor, with the imagination, and with language as elliptical (suggesting recent discussions of the "hermeneutical circle" by way of Heidegger and his turn to speech as poetical). "Philosophy," as Whitehead remarks, "is akin to poetry" (MT 174).

This means that terms such as "eternal objects," "neutrality," "ingression," and "causal efficacy" are metaphors, requiring a "leap of the imagination." Karl Jaspers, whose definition of philosophizing has much in common with that of Whitehead, puts this point well:

Genuine philosophizing consists in watching for that which disappears just beyond thought and thinking. It is watching for what thought conceals just at the boundaries of what it discloses. . . . Philosophy is a reading of the cypher-script of Being through the cypher-script of its own categories. . . . This task of actually taking hold of Being is fulfilled by the symbol (the metaphor or the cypher-status).[2]

Metaphorical language "hovers" (Jaspers's term) on these boundaries; it becomes the "elucidation of existence" (Jaspers), or the descriptive explication of experience (Whitehead and Jung). By extension it becomes the amplification of the archetypes (the child tossing stones in the pool, for Whitehead; the axial crystal, for Jung). Philosophy thus becomes an art form, a metaphorical enactment, the ingression of an eternal object. Where metaphorical enactment drops away, "cognition" takes over. It can only flatten out into "logic," losing its mythos. It "is already mistaken in its roots."[3]

To return now to the suggested parallelism: that Whitehead's eternal objects may be to process as Jung's archetypes are to consciousness.

We note first of all how proximate the notions of "eternal objects" and "archetypes" are to Plato. "We must admit that in some sense or other, we inevitably presuppose this realm of forms," says Whitehead (MT 68). Again: "When Plato thought of mathematics he conceived a changeless world of form. . . . Yet when Plato thought of the realities of action, he swayed to the opposite point of view. He called for 'life and motion' to rescue forms from a meaningless void" (MT 97). It is this appeal to "life and motion" that is central to and often repeated

continuum as if they were spread out on a flat surface, whereas the images of Jung and Hillman suggest excavation of the depths. But Hopper knows that Whitehead is not devoid of a sense of depth, and Jung and Hillman know that depth is not the only dimension of space and time.

If one took the images too literally, one might supppose that the topics investigated were fundamentally different and that the results of the types of investigation could simply be added to one another. That is certainly not Hopper's view. Because it is not mine either, I want to develop the idea that what is imaged as depth in Jung and Hillman is what is imaged as past in Whitehead. Both traditions could be enriched if Whiteheadians realized more fully that the past is the depth of each occasion of human experience, and if Jungians realized that the depth of the psyche is the whole of what Whitehead calls its "actual world." If we all moved freely back and forth between images of depth and images of the temporal past, the power of our imagination would be enhanced.

In Whiteheadian terms, we can roughly correlate the "mental pole" of an occasion of experience, including perception in the mode of presentational immediacy, with its surface. The term surface must not be used derogatively in this context, because mentality is an extremely important aspect of reality. Yet in any occasion of experience it is still a minor part. Overwhelmingly predominant is the physical pole, which corresponds to the experience's depths. The physical pole is the actual world, or the past, as it is constitutive of the present. It is almost entirely, and almost necessarily, unconscious.

Partly because of the flat or lateral images that predominate in Whiteheadian discourse, interpreters of Whitehead have had difficulty in grasping what he says about this pole. As we diagram the situation on the blackboard, the past occasion has a fixed location usually somewhere to the left of the one that is now concrescing. When we speak of its causal efficacy for the concrescing occasion we draw lines between them. The imagery separates the occasion in the past from its causal efficacy in the present. Under the pressure of such images, many Whiteheadians suppose that such efficacy can be exercised only on contiguous occasions, despite Whitehead's contrary view. Others have placed all the agency in the presently concrescing occasion, simply translating "causal efficacy" into "prehension," losing the fundamental intuition of Whitehead that "the many become one," replacing it with the idea that the one constitutes itself out of the many. In this interpretation the past becomes the passive object of present activity.

My point here is that these disastrous changes of Whitehead by some Whitehead scholars are due in part to Whitehead's own images. Whitehead himself was not imprisoned by his flat images, and he followed *deeper* intuitions that broke through the limits the images suggested. But many Whiteheadian scholastics and systematizers are not as free. Hopper's account of Whitehead's images helps us understand where so much of the tradition has gone wrong.

Whiteheadians can overcome some of the bias against attributing causal agency to the *whole* of the past by beginning with images of depth. It is more acceptable in our society to attribute dynamism, power, and activity to the depths than to the past. We can then assert that in every occasion of human experience what is present as its depths is not merely the effects of the past, but the *past itself.*

I speak less confidently of how Jungians would gain if they acknowledged less equivocally that the depth they explore is the whole past of the world as this operates in the present. One possibility is that it would help to overcome tendencies for compartmentalization between the personal and the collective unconscious. It might thereby help overcome ambiguities about the role of culture and the historic possibilities of change in the collective unconscious. It might also help to overcome tendencies toward dichotomizing the inner and the outer. But whether these developments seem advantageous to Jungians, as they do to me, is for them to say.

In any case, I am convinced that what we say, what we mean by what we say, and what we are heard to mean by what we say, are more determined by our images than by our concepts. Incorporating images of depth into the interpretation and development of the Whiteheadian tradition is important not merely to make it more adequate to a range of topics with which Whitehead dealt very little. It is important also for the right understanding of topics with which he dealt extensively.

7

Language as Metaphorical
A Reply to John Cobb

STANLEY R. HOPPER

John Cobb has perceptively isolated a suggestion I ventured to make at the midpoint of my presentation: namely, that "Whitehead's 'eternal objects' (as primordial potentials) are to Whitehead's 'process' as Jung's 'archetypes' are to his 'consciousness.'" He concedes that the parallelism is suggestive, but fears it may lead to a misunderstanding of Whitehead and "distract attention from a suitably Whiteheadian account of archetypes." He later suggests that this is, in his judgment, a weakness in the paper.

Nevertheless, something is at stake here that depends somewhat on the way in which the terms in question are being heard. Cobb is clearly *correct* in his rehearsal of the Whiteheadian terms; but I am raising the question as to whether they might be heard differently. It is not, as Jung once remarked, that we see different things; it is that we see all things differently. Which means, in this instance, that I am speaking neither as a Whiteheadian nor as a Jungian, but rather am trying to explore a zone or an environment in which the two modes of thinking might find some common ground. Jung remarked that he was not a Jungian; and David Bohm has noted that "whoever takes up Whitehead's views is actually taking these as a point of departure, in a further process of the *becoming of knowledge.*"[1]

First off, there is the matter of language. Philosophers, Whitehead indicates at the very beginning of *Process and Reality,* "can never hope finally to formulate these metaphysical first principles." The nature of language "stand[s] in the way." Its elements "remain metaphors mutely continuum as if they were spread out on a flat surface, whereas the images of Jung and Hillman suggest excavation of the depths. But Hopper knows that Whitehead is not devoid of a sense of depth, and Jung and Hillman know that depth is not the only dimension of space and time.

If one took the images too literally, one might supppose that the topics investigated were fundamentally different and that the results of the types of investigation could simply be added to one another. That is certainly not Hopper's view. Because it is not mine either, I want to develop the idea that what is imaged as *depth* in Jung and Hillman is what is imaged as *past* in Whitehead. Both traditions could be enriched if Whiteheadians realized more fully that the past is the depth of each occasion of human experience, and if Jungians realized that the depth of the psyche is the whole of what Whitehead calls its "actual world." If we all moved freely back and forth between images of depth and images of the temporal past, the power of our imagination would be enhanced.

In Whiteheadian terms, we can roughly correlate the "mental pole" of an occasion of experience, including perception in the mode of presentational immediacy, with its surface. The term *surface* must not be used derogatively in this context, because mentality is an extremely important aspect of reality. Yet in any occasion of experience it is still a minor part. Overwhelmingly predominant is the physical pole, which corresponds to the experience's depths. The physical pole is the actual world, or the past, as it is constitutive of the present. It is almost entirely, and almost necessarily, unconscious.

Partly because of the flat or lateral images that predominate in Whiteheadian discourse, interpreters of Whitehead have had difficulty in grasping what he says about this pole. As we diagram the situation on the blackboard, the past occasion has a fixed location usually somewhere to the left of the one that is now concrescing. When we speak of its causal efficacy for the concrescing occasion we draw lines between them. The imagery separates the occasion in the past from its causal efficacy in the present. Under the pressure of such images, many Whiteheadians suppose that such efficacy can be exercised only on contiguous occasions, despite Whitehead's contrary view. Others have placed all the agency in the presently concrescing occasion, simply translating "causal efficacy" into "prehension," losing the fundamental intuition of Whitehead that "the many become one," replacing it with the idea that the one constitutes itself out of the many. In this interpretation the past becomes the passive object of present activity.

My point here is that these disastrous changes of Whitehead by some Whitehead scholars are due in part to Whitehead's own images. Whitehead himself was not imprisoned by his flat images, and he followed *deeper* intuitions that broke through the limits the images suggested. But many Whiteheadian scholastics and systematizers are not as free. Hopper's account of Whitehead's images helps us understand where so much of the tradition has gone wrong.

Whiteheadians can overcome some of the bias against attributing causal agency to the *whole* of the past by beginning with images of depth. It is more acceptable in our society to attribute dynamism, power, and activity to the depths than to the past. We can then assert that in every occasion of human experience what is present as its depths is not merely the effects of the past, but the *past itself.*

I speak less confidently of how Jungians would gain if they acknowledged less equivocally that the depth they explore is the whole past of the world as this operates in the present. One possibility is that it would help to overcome tendencies for compartmentalization between the personal and the collective unconscious. It might thereby help overcome ambiguities about the role of culture and the historic possibilities of change in the collective unconscious. It might also help to overcome tendencies toward dichotomizing the inner and the outer. But whether these developments seem advantageous to Jungians, as they do to me, is for them to say.

In any case, I am convinced that what we say, what we mean by what we say, and what we are heard to mean by what we say, are more determined by our images than by our concepts. Incorporating images of depth into the interpretation and development of the Whiteheadian tradition is important not merely to make it more adequate to a range of topics with which Whitehead dealt very little. It is important also for the right understanding of topics with which he dealt extensively.

7

Language as Metaphorical
A Reply to John Cobb

STANLEY R. HOPPER

John Cobb has perceptively isolated a suggestion I ventured to make at the midpoint of my presentation: namely, that "Whitehead's 'eternal objects' (as primordial potentials) are to Whitehead's 'process' as Jung's 'archetypes' are to his 'consciousness.'" He concedes that the parallelism is suggestive, but fears it may lead to a misunderstanding of Whitehead and "distract attention from a suitably Whiteheadian account of archetypes." He later suggests that this is, in his judgment, a weakness in the paper.

Nevertheless, something is at stake here that depends somewhat on the way in which the terms in question are being heard. Cobb is clearly *correct* in his rehearsal of the Whiteheadian terms; but I am raising the question as to whether they might be heard differently. It is not, as Jung once remarked, that we see different things; it is that we see all things differently. Which means, in this instance, that I am speaking neither as a Whiteheadian nor as a Jungian, but rather am trying to explore a zone or an environment in which the two modes of thinking might find some common ground. Jung remarked that he was not a Jungian; and David Bohm has noted that "whoever takes up Whitehead's views is actually taking these as a point of departure, in a further process of the *becoming of knowledge.*"[1]

First off, there is the matter of language. Philosophers, Whitehead indicates at the very beginning of *Process and Reality,* "can never hope finally to formulate these metaphysical first principles." The nature of language "stand[s] in the way." Its elements "remain metaphors mutely appealing for an imaginative leap" (*PR* 4). The result is that "no language can be anything but elliptical, requiring a leap of the imagination to understand its meaning in its relevance to immediate experience" (*PR* 13). This is where the understanding of Whitehead's philosophy should begin—with metaphor, with the imagination, and with language as elliptical (suggesting recent discussions of the "hermeneutical circle" by way of Heidegger and his turn to speech as poetical). "Philosophy," as Whitehead remarks, "is akin to poetry" (*MT* 174).

This means that terms such as "eternal objects," "neutrality," "ingression," and "causal efficacy" are metaphors, requiring a "leap of the imagination." Karl Jaspers, whose definition of philosophizing has much in common with that of Whitehead, puts this point well:

> Genuine philosophizing consists in watching for that which disappears just beyond thought and thinking. It is watching for what thought conceals just at the boundaries of what it discloses. . . . Philosophy is a reading of the cypher-script of Being through the cypher-script of its own categories. . . . This task of actually taking hold of Being is fulfilled by the symbol (the metaphor or the cypher-status).[2]

Metaphorical language "hovers" (Jaspers's term) on these boundaries; it becomes the "elucidation of existence" (Jaspers), or the descriptive explication of experience (Whitehead and Jung). By extension it becomes the amplification of the archetypes (the child tossing stones in the pool, for Whitehead; the axial crystal, for Jung). Philosophy thus becomes an art form, a metaphorical enactment, the ingression of an eternal object. Where metaphorical enactment drops away, "cognition" takes over. It can only flatten out into "logic," losing its mythos. It "is already mistaken in its roots."[3]

To return now to the suggested parallelism: that Whitehead's eternal objects may be to process as Jung's archetypes are to consciousness.

We note first of all how proximate the notions of "eternal objects" and "archetypes" are to Plato. "We must admit that in some sense or other, we inevitably presuppose this realm of forms," says Whitehead (*MT* 68). Again: "When Plato thought of mathematics he conceived a changeless world of form. . . . Yet when Plato thought of the realities of action, he swayed to the opposite point of view. He called for 'life and motion' to rescue forms from a meaningless void" (*MT* 97). It is this appeal to "life and motion" that is central to and often repeated